THE *SHARESIES* GUIDE TO INVESTING

THE *SHARESIES* GUIDE TO INVESTING

Your roadmap to financial freedom

Brooke Roberts, Leighton Roberts & Sonya Williams

ALLEN&UNWIN
SYDNEY · MELBOURNE · AUCKLAND · LONDON

Please note — investor case-study names have been changed.

First published in 2023
Text © Brooke Roberts, Leighton Roberts and Sonya Williams, 2023

Allen & Unwin
Level 2, 10 College Hill, Freemans Bay
Auckland 1011, New Zealand
Phone: (64 9) 377 3800
Email: auckland@allenandunwin.com
Web: www.allenandunwin.co.nz

83 Alexander Street
Crows Nest NSW 2065, Australia
Phone: (61 2) 8425 0100

A catalogue record for this book is available from
the National Library of New Zealand.

ISBN 978 1 99100 608 0

Design by Megan van Staden
Set in Tiempos 9.5/17
Printed in Australia by the Opus Group

1 3 5 7 9 10 8 6 4 2

Authors' note

As we finish writing this book, it is Sharesies' fifth birthday. Looking back now, no matter how ambitious we were, it would have been hard to imagine how much has changed in that time.

It was once taboo to talk about money; now we have Instagram, TikTok and Facebook communities all dedicated to the subject.

By far most investors used to be male, over 60 and living in the big cities. Now more than 550,000 people have invested billions of dollars in Sharesies and they range from 0 to 97 years old with a representative gender mix.

This is only possible because of the epic mahi (work) of the Sharesies community: the Sharesies team, board, shareholders, advisors, mentors, friends, whānau (family), partners and of course our investors.

We dedicate this book to anyone who imagines a better future for themselves, their whānau and their community.

No matter where you're starting from, you deserve the opportunity to grow your wealth and to ultimately live the life you choose.

Contents

1. The Sharesies story   9

2. Why invest
    (And what is investing, anyway?)   31

3. What to invest in   65

4. What returns can you expect?   105

5. Should you buy local
    or international shares?   131

6. Impact investing:
    how to make a difference   153

7. How to know when to sell   181

8. How to cope with a downturn   205

9. The rest of your financial life   229

10. The end (and the beginning)   251

    Glossary   263

Contents

1.

The Sharesies story

We started Sharesies with one clear goal in mind. We wanted someone with $5 to have the same investment opportunities as someone with $50,000 or $5 million.

We believe that everyone deserves the opportunity to develop their wealth. If the wealthiest people in the world can grow their wealth by investing, why can't those who still have a bit more room to grow?

That might sound like a pretty simple premise. But even in the relatively recent past, things were quite different.

Most people thought investing was something 'other people' did — predominantly rich people who were also male, retired (or nearing it) and living in big cities. That's what the stats showed, too.

Until recently, almost all share trading was arranged through sharebrokers, and it was hard to get in on the action unless you had enough money to make the minimum trade size and justify the brokerage fees. And to get access to extra support or financial advice you needed to have seriously big sums to invest — at least tens of thousands of dollars, but more likely hundreds of thousands.

Sure, there was property investment. Many people have grown up watching others make lots of money from rental properties, and hoped to be able to do the same. But for some the prospect of owning a home to live in is moving further out of reach, let alone buying property as a rental investment.

We looked at the investment landscape and thought it wasn't fair. Doesn't everyone deserve the chance to build their wealth? New technology began to make it all seem possible.

That's where the Sharesies story begins.

A spark of an idea

In 2016, Sonya Williams, who has a background in product and marketing at technology firms, started working for a bank.

She thought she was pretty money savvy, but working in the banking industry showed her she had a lot more to learn.

Sonya wanted to invest and continue to grow her wealth, but she wasn't sure what to do next. She'd been lucky to get into the property market as a homeowner when it was still possible, but prices had shot ahead and the prospect of an investment property was now out of reach.

She started looking for ways to invest but hit dead end after dead end. In many cases, she felt shut down by 'anti-marketing' — instead of trying to lure her in, the message was telling her to go away. Investment opportunities were clearly pitched at a different kind of audience.

At the same time there was a lot of chat going on in the media about the 'generation wars', headlines intended to stoke a 'millennials versus boomers' divide with property at the centre.

Rising house prices were putting pressure on young people, who felt that their parents' generation had had it easier. For their part, some baby boomers were claiming that young people would be better off if they weren't wasting their money on 'luxuries' like takeaway coffee and smashed avocado on toast.

However, it was becoming increasingly obvious that it wasn't just a matter of cutting out brunches to save a bit more money. You could save half your income for years and still not be able to buy a house. Rents were climbing, and it was becoming harder and harder for anyone to save for a house deposit before house prices jumped out of reach again. It was feeling a bit dire for people who were just starting out.

Sonya started to wonder what an alternative might be. There must be another way for people to grow their wealth, outside of what had worked for earlier generations, she thought.

She recalls one night at home with her partner, Ben Crotty, who is a talented creative, designer and illustrator, talking about whether to go out for dinner. They figured it would cost about $50 and Sonya remembers wishing she could do something else with the money.

What if it were possible to invest money quickly, easily and in a really fun way? Imagine if it were as easy to put your money into an investment that would start to build your wealth as it was to order dinner online, or to pop something into the shopping cart on your favourite website?

Sonya started talking about her idea with people at work, and a colleague, John Scully, introduced her to Leighton Roberts.

Leighton had started an investment club as a teenager with friends and family, and they all steadily deposited $50 a week into a joint bank account. When they had saved a decent amount, they started investing. The club started with residential property, because that was what everyone seemed to invest in, then added a sustainable chicken farm, then a commercial property. By the time he met Sonya, Leighton's group was investing almost exclusively in start-up companies. The amount of money they were putting aside each week hadn't changed — they were still contributing $50 a week — but they had been able to pull off some pretty significant investments in the decade or so they had been working together.

For Sonya, it was a revelation.

Not only did it prove that other people also wanted to regularly invest small amounts, it showed that even $50 a week could make a big difference.

It's not about the $50 today — it's about the future value of that $50 once it is invested. And $50 does not have to stay $50 — if you spend it on something that loses value, it can turn into nothing. But if you invest it, it has the potential to be worth much more.

Leighton's experience showed that investing small amounts regularly made sense. Alongside this, Leighton and his then fiancée, now wife, Brooke Roberts, were keen to start their own venture, something that had an impact and combined their experience in product management and finance.

They were keen to get started.

It didn't take long to pull the Sharesies founding team together. Brooke, Leighton, Sonya and Ben were joined by Richard Clark and Martyn Smith, who had been running a technology consulting firm together and had been chatting with Brooke and Leighton about starting a business.

Brooke remembers being captivated by the idea.

She had run businesses when she was in high school, and was involved in a start-up social enterprise. She was already exploring starting a fintech business, too. Sonya's idea seemed a great fit and the group — now the Sharesies co-founders and executive team — thought the time was right. Together, they had most of the key skills they'd need to turn this idea into a business.

Brooke also had experience in the financial services and technology sectors, and could see how inaccessible that world was to many people. She agreed that whether you have $5 or $5 million, you should have the same opportunities to make money.

Brooke remembers the exciting early days of bringing the team together: 'We are the sort of people who like to solve problems and we could all see that a lack of investment opportunities was a real problem for younger people in particular. There was a real opportunity to make a big difference in Aotearoa New Zealand and around the world.

'It was exciting to see everyone in the room getting hyped about the prospect. But anyone who has had anything to do with a start-up business will know that it's not enough to think you've got a good idea and psych each other up to ever-increasing levels of excitement. Other people have to be into it, too.

'The difference between a cool idea and a really viable business is that other people have the problem and you build the right solution to fix it for them.

'That's why we took it out to testing, asking other people what they thought.'

Asking the market

Before officially launching anything, we (Sonya, Brooke and Leighton) went through a customer validation process, taking around six months to talk to anyone we could find, whenever and wherever we could.

We surveyed groups of people about their views on money, what they thought about investing, whether they wanted to invest, how they perceived investment markets and their financial plans, as well as broader questions about their lives and their goals for the future.

We continuously refined our idea, and tested it every couple of weeks by talking to different people.

Through that process, we discovered that most people had a really negative relationship with money, even though it was a big part of their lives. Money and health are two things in life that really stay at the front of your mind when they're not going well. Most people were members of KiwiSaver (New Zealand's superannuation savings scheme) but they didn't really think of that as an investment.

Almost all the people we spoke with said they wanted to be investors — being an investor meant you were savvy with money and were trying to get ahead, they reckoned — but they just weren't doing it.

Why not? Three main reasons emerged.

- They were priced out. This means they did not have the minimum investment required to get started.
- They were jargoned out. Financial services and investment markets are great at using technical language that can be hard to understand. Technical language can put people off and make them think they have too much to learn before they can even start.
- They were branded out. This means they did not feel the investments available met their needs as an investor. This made sense because most investments being offered at the time were pitched at people approaching retirement.

We also discovered there was a stigma about investing. At the time, only about 20 per cent of New Zealanders owned shares, and most of them were older men living in Auckland. The story wasn't much better in Australia.

There was an obvious undercurrent of a desire to invest being blocked by a lack of opportunities to do so. This gave us the motivation and confidence we needed to commit to making Sharesies happen. Everyone deserves the opportunity to grow their wealth. That belief was our starting point and, while we all thought it should be true, there was some work to do to make it a reality.

We decided to create an online platform where you could invest whatever amount you chose, big or small, and we wanted it to be fun, informative and easy to use.

But our bigger dream was to create a financially empowered generation. We imagined a future where there was an even playing field, where no one had the upper hand over anyone else just because they understood the mysterious world of investing and other people didn't. We didn't want some people to be stuck slogging away getting small returns from money saved in a bank account while others were cashing in on high-returning and high-risk assets like shares or properties.

We wanted to create a future where people approached financial decisions with hopefulness and optimism, not negativity. We wanted money to be seen as the means, not the end.

What does this mean? Well, while money plays a big part in how people live their lives and the dreams they can achieve, the bigger prize is the self-actualisation — in other words, the personal fulfilment and reaching of potential — that can happen when people feel in control of their decisions.

How empowered would you feel if you didn't have to worry

about money? If all your financial planning was a positive experience?

We wanted to give people a tool to help them to live the life they want. We hoped to make it easy to do the right thing in a system that can sometimes feel like it's designed to trip you up. We wanted everyone's money to be in the best possible place to achieve their financial goals.

Getting started

Once we decided we were going to go for it, things happened pretty quickly. Almost by chance, we'd developed a group of founders with the range of skills needed to build our business and find the solutions we were looking for.

Martyn and Richard were both from technical backgrounds, and knew how to build the architecture for an investor platform. Brooke and Leighton were in the banking and finance world and had experience with starting and running businesses. Sonya had experience in scaling tech start-ups in product and marketing and Ben was from a creative industry background and knew how to connect people with a new idea. That was really important because one of the biggest risks we faced was that the idea wouldn't resonate with people because they thought that money wasn't their thing, or that being an investor wasn't for them. We had learned that one of the biggest reasons why people weren't investing was that it wasn't 'connecting' with them, so making the concept relevant for potential investors was going to be a huge part of whether our business was a success.

People definitely raised some eyebrows at our business having six founders, but it's only now that we look back and realise we actually had everything we needed to create the platform and get it to market. For our idea to work we needed to be a technology company, a finance company and a creative company (we now call that a 'funtech'). On top of that, the timing was right for each of us, given our ages and stage of life, for the idea to take off.

Hold on! What does Sharesies actually do?

If you haven't encountered us yet, we'd better explain what Sharesies actually is.

Sharesies is a wealth-development platform that allows you to invest, no matter how much, or how little, money or investing experience you have. We enable you to invest in listed companies, managed funds and exchange-traded funds from all over the world, with no minimum investment required, even if that means you're only buying a fraction of a share at a time.

To be a viable business, Sharesies needs to make some money, too. We do this mainly through fees when you buy or sell most investments, exchange currency, top up with a card or transfer shares. We also earn interest on any money in your Sharesies account (called a 'wallet') that you haven't yet invested. Lastly, some fund providers pay us to list their funds on Sharesies.

As Sharesies has grown, so has the range of people investing through us — Sharesies investors are aged from 0 to 97, and have between $5 and $5 million in their portfolios.

Counting down

We were up and running within eight months.

Our initial meetings were in October 2016, and in February

2017, we began to work in the business full time.

It was a huge move to give up a reliable source of income for what was, at that point, still an idea, but our employers gave us extended leave, which was really supportive of them and reduced the risk a bit. In reality, however, we all knew we weren't going back. We were 100 per cent in.

It sounds scary to launch into a business like that but to us, it felt even more risky not to do it. The research showed us that there was a real need for what Sharesies had to offer.

When you're a problem-solver sort of person, like we all are, once you hear about a problem and see that by solving it you could have a big impact, you can't walk away. We knew we had to lean into the idea because if it could happen, it would be amazing.

We could see how different the world would look if people were financially empowered — and once you have that sort of vision in your mind, you can't look away.

We were all people who couldn't look away.

Sharesies' first website launched just before Christmas 2016. At that stage we were just testing the branding and idea out on the market; we weren't offering any investment opportunities.

This approach allowed us to refine what we were doing by taking our ideas and testing the market, then refining them a bit more and testing again.

We met with regulators to understand the rules we needed to meet and started picking the brains of people who could help us. A great thing about starting a business in New Zealand is that people are really accessible. Lots of people we spoke with thought it was strange that something like Sharesies wasn't already in the market, or said they wished they'd thought of it first.

Some people weren't convinced we could pull it off. Someone

said to us that they didn't think we'd get to 10,000 investors —
but by the end of 2017 we were at 10,000 and in 2020, we reached
250,000.

There were a few investors in Wellington who were interested
in backing us so we started a capital raise on a convertible note — a
type of short-term loan that converts into an equity investment —
because we didn't want to try to value the business before it had
any revenue. We set out to raise $200,000 to get us off the ground
but ended up with $400,000 from investors and supportive friends
and family. People also joined a waitlist through our website so they
could be involved when we were ready to go live.

Before we even launched, we had 6000 people on that list
without any marketing or promotion. That was a huge moment, a
real signal for us that Sharesies might be something great. If people
don't think they have the problem that you're offering to solve, your
first job is to convince them that they need you. But it was obvious
from that waitlist that the problem was there and people wanted
help from us to fix it.

We launched to a closed group in June 2017 with access to six
exchange-traded funds (ETFs) and it took off from there. We were
underway!

Power in numbers

When you think of a typical start-up, you probably imagine a couple
of guys who dream up a product in their garage and bring it to
market.

Our start-up looked a bit different — there were six of us
working together, all co-founders and now taking roles in the
executive at Sharesies.

Some people struggled to understand how having six co-founders would work. We were doing things quite differently to a traditional start-up, challenging a lot of assumptions along the way.

But looking back now, the fact that there has been a group of us has been a real key to our success. For example, some businesses fail if the founders fall out but we have developed a way of working that feels quite different. We aren't ego-based in our decision-making — it's not my idea versus your idea, because there are so many of us. The best idea wins.

We decided early on that we needed to sit down and talk about the type of business that we were creating. What did we want it to be like to work at Sharesies? What did we want to do? We spent lots of time talking, and settled on some values that still guide us today.

These values are:

- 'chasing remarkable' — always striving to create a better future, being bold and taking risks, challenging the status quo and believing in ourselves;
- 'in it together' — harnessing the power of our team and looking for how we do things together; and
- 'always care' — showing care for ourselves, each other, our investors, our stakeholders and the work we do.

The compounding impact that happens when you act out of care is amazing. We didn't initially intend to spend so much time working on the goals and planning for the business, and it probably wouldn't have happened if there had just been a couple of us. But doing this work has given us a very strong foundation for our future success. We have been able to build Sharesies in the way we intended. We now have a team of more than 200 people and we still have the same values. Our values grow with us as we grow and each team member makes a huge contribution.

We're also a Certified B Corp, which is something we're really proud and excited about. B Corp stands for 'Better Corporation' and is a global accreditation for companies that are designed for purpose and profit — companies that have a desire to reduce inequality, lower poverty levels, create a healthier environment and build stronger communities. We're really passionate about these goals and we believe other businesses should strive for them, too. We hope to see this being the norm in the future.

What's next?

We've been up and running for a while now, but we aren't slowing down from here.

We consider Sharesies to be a wealth-development platform, not just for investing. We want to help people grow their wealth as they move through the milestones of their lives. We hope that this helps improve financial inclusiveness and ultimately equality in society.

Our ultimate goal is to help people grow their wealth so they can live the life they choose. We have done a lot to help people get started but now we want to do more, helping people to have confidence in their investments and to feel motivated to keep going.

We are setting up Sharesies around the world, starting with Australia and looking to other markets beyond that, too. If more people get into investing, then there will be an increase in general investor knowledge and education. It's cool to see people linking what is going on in business and in the wider world with how that can affect their investment portfolio, and starting to understand how it all interconnects and helps to build their wealth over time.

We have always known there was so much opportunity in this area, but as Sharesies has grown and celebrated success, we have been able to take a few moments to sit and reflect, and to enjoy it. But as founders we can see there is so much more to do to create financial empowerment for everyone.

We have fun and make a point of enjoying our work. We reckon that if someone doesn't enjoy making a meal, you can taste it in the food, and a big part of what we do is making something enjoyable, creating a positive relationship between people and money, and giving people a chance to throw away any negative emotions they might have about it.

It's hard work but it's really worth it.

We can see a better future, and empowering people to invest is a big part of that

Our purpose is becoming more and more important because financial inequality is growing. Inequality is often measured by something called the Gini coefficient, which takes all incomes into account. A score of 0 indicates complete equality, where everyone earns the same, and a score of 100 would mean one household has all the income. New Zealand and Australia have a Gini coefficient of about 33. At the end of the 1980s, it was more like 26.

There's also a generational wealth divide — a recent survey by Deloitte[1] found that two thirds of millennials and Gen Zs think wealth and income is unequally distributed between the

---

1   'The Deloitte Global Millennial Survey: A decade in review', https://www2.deloitte.com/content/dam/Deloitte/global/Documents/2021-deloitte-global-millennial-survey-report.pdf

generations. A recent Australian survey[2] showed that baby boomers, a quarter of that country's population, owned more than half the nation's wealth, even though younger people were starting to earn some pretty decent incomes.

It's all because asset prices have increased, while wages and other forms of income have not. People who've owned assets (like houses) have become richer and richer over the years, while those who are still saving are left behind.

That's become even more obvious in recent years. You may have heard about the 'K-shaped' recovery out of Covid-19 lockdowns. People who owned assets became a lot richer as asset values rose, but everyone else was left struggling. We don't think that's fair and we want to do what we can to help.

We weren't investing pros. You don't need to be, either

If you take anything away from this potted history of Sharesies and our beliefs and values, we hope it's that you — whoever you are — have just as much right and ability to develop your wealth as anyone else. We knew a bit about investing but we weren't expert investors when we began. Here's a rundown on our investing backgrounds:

Sonya

Sonya had grown up with some good money management and advice from her parents and wider family, and was taught about the value of a dollar — what you do with what you get — and the difference between

---

2   'Australia's generations by wealth and income', nmpeducation
     (website), https://www.nmpeducation.com.au/opinions/australias-
     generations-wealth-income

buying an asset versus what was just spending. She picked up some shares through her work at Xero (Xero Limited ASX:XRO) and other start-ups but initially she didn't fully understand what that meant.

Sonya always felt self-conscious about money and numbers, even after studying accounting and having a career in finance and technology companies. Now she loves that she gets to make the money and investing world a little bit more accessible and to help make growing your wealth feel empowering. After all, knowing how to find an answer is more important than knowing the answer. Financial knowledge is within your reach and you can learn more about it, one day at a time.

Over the years Sonya's confidence about finance and investing has grown. She loves being an investor and invests regularly, personally and through investment clubs. She invests in things that interest her and align with her values including listed companies, start-ups and art.

Brooke

Brooke had grown up seeing how money could create opportunities — on her dad's side of the family, money was much more of a struggle as he managed alone with five children. Her mother, for whom Brooke is an only child, found it easier financially to offer Brooke an array of opportunities.

When Brooke was at high school, she became really interested in business, economics and how investments work. She completed a Master's degree in finance but was making investments in people rather than shares at that time. She used the money she had available to pay for her sister to go to boarding school and to support her brother while he lived with her.

She really wanted to be an investor in the traditional sense and had friends who were in investment groups, or whose families had sharebrokers. She signed up to a broking service intending to buy shares that way, but didn't want to pay the brokerage fee for the small amount of money she planned to invest.

When she went to work at Xero (Xero Limited ASX:XRO) she was given shares as part of her remuneration, which became her first traditional investment.

Brooke didn't start investing regularly until Sharesies was launched and she began building her investment portfolio. As she watched it grow, she learnt about her risk appetite. Now, she also invests in start-ups, which can be risky but rewarding, and focuses on impact investing — knowing that her money is working towards creating the future she wants to see.

Leighton

Leighton had developed an investing history through his investment club, which meant he invested a small amount regularly and harnessed the power of time. His mum and her siblings invested in commercial property, and that was the spark for Leighton to start an investment club with friends and family (his three brothers, mum, dad, cousins, aunties and uncles all came on board).

Despite this history of direct investing, Leighton still made his first investments into managed funds and exchange-traded funds through Sharesies.

Leighton grew up in Hāwera, South Taranaki, and was very active in the Young Enterprise Scheme at high school, 'by far the best education experience I had at school,' he says. He took a roundabout path to a finance career, starting his full-time working life as a trumpet player for the New Zealand Army Band, while studying for a finance degree extramurally. Even so, he had no doubt that entrepreneurship and finance were in his future.

Investing is not just where you put your money but where you put your time — investing in yourself is probably a big part of your journey, too. When you learn something, your wealth of knowledge increases, and that puts you in a better position for future success. You are your own biggest asset.

We're here to help you get underway — and we believe, whoever you are, that you can do it.

People often underestimate the power of believing they can do something. There is a stereotype that Australians and New Zealanders are bad at saving and investing. The danger of stereotypes is that people start to believe them, so they become self-fulfilling prophecies.

People hear that they are bad at something and stop believing they can do it. But every builder's apprentice has their first day at work, and no one expects them to build a house on day one.

When you take down the smoke and mirrors of what an 'expert' is, it's just someone who kept doing something. Just start — have your first day — and see where your journey takes you from there.

Some of the best feedback we have had so far has been from the people who say that our investment platform has given them hope.

So set a goal, keep going, accept a stumble every now and again, and don't give up. Throughout the rest of this book, we'll show you how to set yourself up for a brighter financial future.

Investor story: In from the start

Sarah (Te Ātiawa ki Te Whakarongotai) was one of Sharesies' first investors. The now-32-year-old's partner was friends with Brooke and Leighton, who mentioned their plans to start an investment platform.

Sarah remembers looking at her savings account and feeling frustrated. 'Nothing was happening with it.'

Her mother had given her a book about the importance of women having independent financial plans and building their own wealth. 'I heard about Sharesies and I thought I would give it a go, mainly because it just seemed really user friendly and not scary. I had thought investing meant I had to go into a big hedge fund scheme or something and I wouldn't know where to find that. I wouldn't have even known what to search for on the internet.'

Sarah said Sharesies was the first place that she had heard of that was tailored to investors like herself rather than to people with lots of money to invest. She started with $10 and then set up a regular payment of $20 a week. 'I just had a play with it.'

The amount that she's invested has changed over the years. 'It bounced around a bit through having babies and things like that.'

While Sharesies has since expanded its offering of investments, Sarah has stuck with the initial exchange-traded funds that she has put money in since the beginning. 'There are so many more options now — at the time it was perfect for me because there were just six options.'

Sarah said a lot of her friends were putting their money

into the Smartshares Australian Resources ETF (Exchange Traded Fund), but she had opted not to because she was concerned about the impact of those investments on climate change. 'I picked a whole lot of New Zealand investments. The Smartshares NZ Top 50 ETF was and still is my main fund. Looking at it now, I think I should really start investigating other options, but I haven't yet.'

While her partner has spread his investments over a wide range of funds and direct investments, Sarah has been happy with the results delivered by her initial investment choices.

It's been nice to know that the money is there if she needs it, but Sarah said she hasn't ever withdrawn anything from her Sharesies account. 'I have a savings account as well for when I need flights or urgent car repairs and stuff. It would have to be quite serious to take it out of my Sharesies account. My idea is that's my long-term plan.'

The Sharesies effect has rubbed off on other parts of her life, too. Sarah said she had never paid much attention to her KiwiSaver account until she started investing via Sharesies.

'I thought they would all be the same but doing Sharesies on my own and seeing the returns I could get, when I saw the returns of my provider I thought that was quite average for how much money was in there and that caused me to investigate other funds. If it wasn't for Sharesies, I would have thought that must be what everyone was getting and just carried on.'

Sarah's daughter now also has a Sharesies account, to which Sarah and her partner contribute $10 each a week. 'She's got quite a bit of money, I reckon, for a two-year-old.

My partner manages that one. I don't look at it very often —
he has so much fun.'

Sarah says she feels much more financially empowered
through her experience of being a Sharesies investor. 'I feel
almost smug now when I see articles about trying to get
young people to invest. I feel really proud that I'm doing
that — that I have money in different places and I'm trying
to make it grow. It feels like I'm setting myself up in the right
way. I feel really good about that.'

2.

Why invest? (And what is investing, anyway?)

F irst things first. What is investing, anyway?

Very simply, 'investing' is when you allocate something (usually money, but it could also be your time or efforts) with the goal of getting some sort of gain (income or profit) from it. (You could also describe this as 'making money'.) Most of the time, buying a car isn't investing because a car is likely to decrease in value over the time you own it. But when you put your money into shares, you usually expect them to be worth more in the future than they are now (although they may go up and down), and you might get some income (dividends) from the shares while you hold them, too.

What is a 'share'? Well, when you invest in a company, you take ownership of a piece of that company, known as a share. Company owners might decide to put a portion of their company up for sale by listing it if they want to raise money, maybe for growth plans or because they want some reward for the work they have put in. People buy those shares because they think the money will be worth more in the long term, either because the company will grow and become more valuable, or they will be paid dividends along the way. (More on that in a minute.)

So, why might you want to invest?

The reasons people decide to start investing — whether it's in shares, funds, a business of their own or investment property — vary a lot.

Some people want to set themselves up for a comfortable retirement at some point in the distant future. Others want to build up their wealth for a specific purpose, or to have a nest egg available to them in case they need it. Some people want financial freedom — to build up enough investments that they no longer have to have a 'day job'. The reason behind why you want to invest is as unique as you are, and is up to you.

Most fundamentally, though, people usually invest because they want to grow their wealth, and to put themselves or their families in a better position for the future. They aren't happy with the status quo and want to do something more with what they have.

Sometimes (and this is a big one among our investors), investors also want to see better outcomes for the wider world.

For these people, investing is not just about creating wealth for themselves — it's about trying to make a difference. Our investors tell us that it's hard for them to picture their financial future without thinking about the type of world they want to live in. They want to use their money to back something that's really important to them. You often see this philosophy in start-up companies seeking money from supporters, or in businesses that come into the market with a new way of doing things, which attracts investment support.

Because everyone has their eyes on a better future, we find the investing world is generally a pretty happy and optimistic place. Although there are ups and downs, people who think everything is going downhill from here don't usually invest, because they can't see how things might turn out well. Getting involved with investing means you're surrounding yourself with people who can not only imagine something better, but are doing their bit to make it happen.

Before you start

The very first thing to do is to get rid of the idea that you have to be a financial mastermind before you can start investing in shares.

Everyone can be an investor, no matter what level of knowledge or money you're starting with. We all start somewhere and you are just as entitled to get involved, whether it's your first time, or you have some investing experience under your belt.

We all know from other areas in our lives about the power of learning by doing. It's all fine and well watching from the sidelines, but the real learning comes when we're the ones on the field. The experience of investing, even with just a couple of dollars, is the same. Getting involved will give you invaluable knowledge of how investing works, so you are set up for more success as you continue on your wealth journey. Your investment earns the same return whether it's $1 or $1,000,000.

Some people avoid investing out of fear of 'getting it wrong' but really, there isn't a right or wrong answer when it comes to investing. There is only what's right for you and your circumstances.

There isn't a specific formula for success. Ditch the idea that investing is a zero-sum game and there are winners and losers. It's not binary, and the 'right' or 'wrong' decision isn't static. What might look like the wrong choice one day could be the best investment you have ever made the next, or something considered a 'sure thing' could hit an unexpected rough patch.

When you're getting into something new, it can feel a bit like you've walked into a room where a movie is playing, it's halfway through and there's no one to whisper the plot to you to help you understand what's going on and how everything fits together. We're here to help you fill in the gaps and take you through some of the things to consider so you can build the investment portfolio and strategy that's right for you.

Investor story: The long game

Ryan knew nothing about shares or investing when he started out in January 2018. 'It's been a slow process learning about shares, managed funds and exchange-traded funds,' he says. He puts a bit of money into his account each week and has achieved an overall return so far of more than 15 per cent since making his initial investment. 'For me, it's a long game.'

Getting in the habit

We've been really deliberate about setting Sharesies up in a way that makes it easy to invest a set amount every week, fortnight or whatever works for you. Some people invest very small amounts of money while others invest significant lump sums.

This is because we firmly believe that like exercising, creating habits around money is one of the best things you can do.

Investing regularly, such as every payday, is a really popular investing strategy known as dollar-cost averaging.

As you know, a share's price can go up and down depending on what people perceive the value of the share to be at a point in time. With a dollar-cost averaging investing strategy, you choose an amount to invest into a certain share and do this on a regular basis. Because you're buying the same investment every time at different prices, sometimes you may end up buying it when it's expensive and sometimes when it's cheap. Over time the price will even out (or 'average out', to link it back to its name).

Sometimes human nature can work against us when it comes to making financial decisions. For example, sometimes it's really easy to follow the crowd. This can lead us to wanting to invest in the same way as other people — so when a share price is rising, we're more attracted to buy, and when the price is falling, we want to sell (or are less interested in buying, at least).

But in reality, unless there is some new information that has changed your perception of the long-term value of that investment, or your personal circumstances have changed, you sticking with your strategy and continuing to invest through a price dip, will lower the average price you've paid over time.

Buying regularly means you see price changes more often. Being able to observe these fluctuations in share prices may mean you're less likely to panic when the prices drop, because you've become aware of how the value of shares change week to week, day to day and even hour to hour. And where you do buy low, hopefully you'll benefit from those low prices later. This means you can take the pressure off from feeling you need to 'time the market'.

A big part of investing is building the habit of being engaged with what is happening in the economy and how it might affect your portfolio. One of the best things you can do for your future self is to create great money habits right from the beginning.

How human behaviour affects our financial decisions (and how to overcome it)

Investing success isn't just about the numbers — a big part of making it work is how you behave.

Some behaviours are things that will really empower you to achieve your goals if you get them right — things like getting into a habit and sticking with it no matter what, or having an optimistic outlook and focusing on the long-term potential of your investment.

But there are things that you need to watch for — things like confirmation bias, where you get stuck in a bubble of only looking for opinions you agree with, which may mean you miss out on opportunities; and herding (sometimes called FOMO), where you make a decision because everyone else is doing it.

The good news is that keeping unhelpful instincts in check can make a really big, beneficial difference to your ultimate outcome — and it's all up to you. We'll explain more, and give you some practical tips, in Chapter 4.

How much is the right amount to invest?

It's really up to you. If you're creating a habit, think of an amount you think you can stick to on a regular basis — something that's high enough to help you reach your goal, but low enough that you don't constantly raid your investments when you need spending money for coffee, beers or anything else that would be tempting enough for you to hit the withdraw button.

You could invest a dollar a day or $200, but it needs to work for you. The main thing is that whatever amount you choose is affordable and sustainable, and you can stick with it over time. Investing $5 every week for a year ends up with a bigger investment than a one-off deposit of $50, and your investment fund will build up more quickly than you think.

How much are you willing to let your day-to-day standard of living change in order to meet your investment goals? One end of the spectrum would be investing nothing at all, while the other extreme would be living on nothing but two-minute noodles, investing every dollar you make until you hit your investment target. We reckon it's better to invest a smaller affordable amount that you can stick to, rather than invest a large amount, then stop investing once you get sick of noodles.

If you have a clear goal you are working towards, whether that's $5000 or $500,000, that goal will guide the amount you need to invest.

The longer you have to reach your goal, the less you have to put aside each week to reach it, and vice versa. If you want to buy a house in 10 years, you don't need to invest as much each week as you would if you wanted to buy a house in five years.

Maybe you don't have a set goal in mind. That's OK — the same principles apply. Think of an amount you can manage to invest regularly and start with that.

An investment in shares is a bit illiquid — that means it's a bit slower to turn into spendable cash than if it were sitting in a bank account (because you'd have to sell the shares and wait for the money to come through before you could spend it). Some people use this as a strategy for them to stick to their financial goals, in the same way that you might rid your house of junk food when you're going on a diet.

Run the numbers

Let's assume you make about $50,000 a year. After tax, that's roughly $800 a week. And let's also say your goal is to build your investment to $100,000.

The key things that determine when you'll hit your goal are how much you can afford to invest, and the percentage return your investment makes.

For example, if you were to invest $200 per week, you'd hit your goal of $100,000 in eight years — providing the average return is 7 per cent per annum. If your investment returns 2 per cent per annum, you'll hit your goal within nine years and if it doesn't make a return, you'll hit your goal within 10 years. It's important to remember that past returns aren't an indicator of future returns, so you might find that your investment goes up and down year to year and doesn't hit the same performance as the year before.

But $200 per week can be quite a bit for some households. It might be more sustainable to extend your timeframe, and invest less money each week. If you decided to invest $100 per week instead, you would reach your goal in 13 years (with 7 per cent per annum returns), 17 years (with 2 per cent per annum returns), or 20 years (if you don't make a return).

Ultimately, it's up to you how you trade off the speed to reach your goal with what is sustainable for you to settle on an investment amount.

Fill the gaps

Let's say you decided to invest $100 a week. That means that from your $800 a week salary, you're living off $700 a week. Now let's say you get a new job, and your pay increases from $50,000 to $60,000 a year. Your weekly pay goes up as well, to around $925 a week.

Before your pay rise, you were happily living off $700 a week. Your expenses probably haven't changed, but your income has. You could start investing more to fill the gaps. You could invest $225 a week, and continue to live off $700. That's more than doubling your weekly investment, without affecting your standard of living.

Filling the gaps is great for increasing the amount you invest, but you might want to spend some of your money on yourself. Fair enough. After all, you worked for that pay rise.

So instead of filling the gaps, you could decide to invest a percentage of your income.

If you decide to invest 10 per cent of your weekly pay, and you make $800 a week, then you'll start out by investing $80 a week. When you get that $10,000 pay rise, and your pay goes up to $925 a week, you'll invest $92.50 each week. You invest more, but you also get to reward yourself with more money to spend each payday.

Set your own strategy

You will probably get lots of helpful advice from friends and family when you are starting out, as well as from online chat groups and social media. But don't lose sight of your personal investment objectives and financial plan.

What are you trying to achieve with your investments? Why are you making them? Which companies or funds do you think have the brightest future? When you're starting out, it's tempting to follow the advice of people who seem to know more than you. But you'll be on much firmer ground if you've worked out what you want from your investments so you can decide what fits the bill.

Sometimes, it might help to ask others why they are making their investment choices. Having a deeper conversation about this context will help you assess if their decisions are relevant for your situation.

About a third of investors[3] say they've jumped into an investment because they didn't want to miss out — which can be a bit of a worry if you don't know why everyone else is doing it.

The problem with following someone else's strategy is that it can be hard to make changes as you go along. If you don't know why you did something in the first place, whether that's investing in a certain investment or choosing to invest a certain amount of money, it can be hard to assess whether you want to stick with it if your circumstances or the investment environment change.

Remember, there's no such thing as a dumb question when it comes to investing. Companies and fund managers want your money and it's their job to provide you with all the information that you need to make an informed decision. And while they can provide you with the information you need, they might not be able to give you financial advice. So if you find you do need some extra help to make your decisions, consider contacting a financial advisor.

The magic of compounding

One of the great reasons to start investing as soon as you can is the magic of compounding.

This is one of the most important messages we hope you'll get from reading this book. When it comes to investing, the value of time in the market can play an enormous part in your investment success.

If someone told you there was a way to get extra money by doing nothing, you'd probably be pretty sceptical. But let us introduce you to the power of compounding.

---

3   'Jumping into that investment? Take a mo and think about it', FMA (website), https://www.fma.govt.nz/news-and-resources/fma-stories/ jumping-into-that-investment-take-a-mo-and-think-about-it/

Magic of Compounding
Starting early vs. starting late

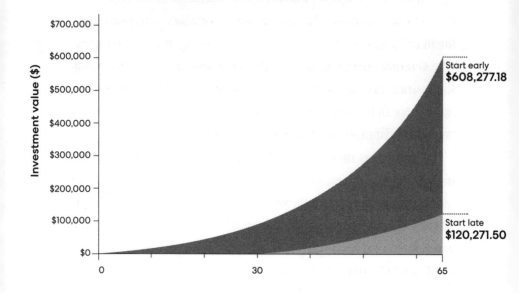

* Based on a $25 per week investment with a 5% annual return. Graph not representative of share market volatility. Results are hypothetical and don't represent the performance of any individual investment. Numbers prepared by Sharesies Limited.

It's best explained like this. Let's say you invest $1000 in your first year. You make a 7 per cent return, giving you $1070 in your account. The next year, you make another 7 per cent, but you make it on the $1070 (the initial amount invested plus the returns reinvested), not just the initial $1000. At the end of year two, you end up with $1144.90, without having put any more of your own money in at all. Returns on investment can fluctuate year to year (and sometimes can go down) but assuming the returns continue like this year after year, you'll soon be making significant amounts just from the returns on your returns — not counting the money you're continuing to contribute yourself.

You can earn compound interest when you reinvest the returns from any bank account that pays interest, term deposits, shares and managed funds.

Compounding works its magic most dramatically when it has a long time to do it. If you start investing at a young age, the amount you have to save to reach a goal is substantially less than the amount you need if you start later in life.

In many ways, time is as great an asset for investors as the money itself.

If you are 20 and could earn a 5 per cent return per year, you would only need to save $120 a week to give you $1 million by the time you are 65. Around $725,000 of that $1 million would be from compound returns.

A 40-year-old would need to put aside just under $400 a week to reach that same goal, and only about $489,000 of the final $1 million would come from compound returns.

In a world where home ownership is becoming more difficult, the pension age looks likely to increase and we're being encouraged to plan to fund our own retirements, the idea that young people might have an advantage (time!) is refreshing. We must create financial independence for ourselves in order to live the lifestyles we choose, and can use the power of compounding interest to do it.

When you are saving or investing, compounding works in your favour. But be aware that when you borrow, compounding is your enemy. It works the same way but in the opposite direction — the longer you hold the debt, the more you'll pay in interest.

A women's issue?

We think it's really important to set yourself up to make the most of your money, no matter your gender identity.

But for this section, we're keen to spend a moment digging into the particular issues that play a part when it comes to women and investing.

Generally, women earn less than men — the gender pay gap is real, and it isn't dropping quickly. Studies show women also tend to have more time out of the workforce looking after children and other family members. They also tend to live longer than men, so they have a longer retirement period to fund. And if a relationship breaks up, it's usually the women who come out worse off financially.

Women do have an investing superpower — studies show that women are better at buying and holding their investments than men rather than chopping and changing.[4] Women are also less likely to sell an investment in a panic, but they're also more likely to make conservative investments which earn lower returns.

Women's outcomes are not helped by a lot of financial information being aimed at men — one study in the UK found almost three quarters of money articles aimed at men were about investing but 90 per cent of articles aimed at women were about spending less.[5]

We're not sharing this because it is all doom and gloom, but to show you the importance of planning how you will keep your

---

4   'Women investors are still outperforming men, study finds', CNBC (website), https://www.cnbc.com/2021/10/11/women-investors-are-still-outperforming-men-study-finds.

5   "Media stereotype women in financial coverage, study finds', The Guardian (website), https://www.theguardian.com/money/2018/mar/10/media-stereotype-women-in-financial-coverage-study-finds

financial goals on track, whether you're single or coupled-up, and even if you are out of the workforce for a while. It's important to get stuck in even if it feels like the investment world isn't always made with you in mind. We think it's going to get better!

Here are a few things you can do:

- Back yourself and your ability — you can be an investor, even if you're just getting started. Yes, historically the investing world has been mostly male, but this is changing. At Sharesies, 48 per cent of our investors identify as women.
- Talk about money and share your knowledge — often it's not knowing or talking about money that stops people learning. Talk to the women in your life about money and investing (this doesn't have to mean sharing the figures). Such valuable information is exchanged when we talk and ask questions together.
- Encourage other women and girls in your life — girls are often excluded from financial conversations when they are growing up, which means they don't learn about context for investment decisions. Representation matters, and encouragement from others is hugely helpful as we start on the investment journey.

Investor story: Staying engaged

Iris began investing with Sharesies when her boss gave her a gift voucher as a leaving present. 'It turned out to be a great introduction to being more involved with my portfolio's performance,' she says. Previously Iris had bought and held investments without tracking how they were performing. 'With Sharesies, I'm much more engaged in watching my holdings grow.'

The best time to start? Right now

The best time to plant a tree was 20 years ago. The second best time is now.
— Chinese proverb

It can be tempting to try to find the perfect moment to get started, but the reality is it's really hard to forecast share prices accurately. Even professionals whose job it is to know these things get it wrong almost as often as they get it right.

Instead of trying to time the market for the maximum returns, holding back and waiting for a bargain, you're better off to focus on time *in* the market, and to start as soon as you can. Over time, your returns will change, even if it turns out that you bought at what looks at the time like a bad point. Think about people who bought their first house 30 years ago, perhaps your parents, or some older people you know. Chances are, they bought their first property for what seems today like an insanely small amount of money. But that amount could have been quite high by the standards of the time. It's time in the market that makes it seem like they got a serious bargain all those years ago.

We can avoid the desire to time the market by thinking about what the particular company we are buying shares in might be doing in 10 years' time. Do we believe in what the company is doing? Will the world in 10 years be a world in which this company is successful? What else needs to be true for that to be the case?

Looking years ahead takes the heat off trying to time the market because you're backing the business's fundamentals, not trying to pick the short-term changes.

Then, when we listen to the news, we can think about whether what's happening in the world ties into the hypothesis we have for how our investments will perform, but we don't have to get hung up on every market movement. We're engaging with what's going on but not out of a frantic need to buy and sell — we're just keeping an eye on whether what's happening is what we would hope to see for a company we're backing.

Sticking and having confidence in your strategy is a winner over the latest hot tip any day.

What kind of investor are you?

New Zealand's Financial Markets Authority did some research on people using investment platforms like Sharesies and decided there were four key types of investors.[6]

Although we don't often fit neatly into boxes, it might be

------

6   'DIY investors encouraged to "take a mo" before giving in to FOMO', FMA (website), https://www.fma.govt.nz/news-and-resources/ media-releases/diy-investors-encouraged-to-take-a-mo-before-giving-in-to-fomo/

helpful to use these descriptions to think about what category you fit in, and what that might mean for the way you choose to invest your money.

Speculators

About 20 per cent of people investing are speculators, having a go and letting their investments take them on an emotional journey. Speculators think taking a risk is how you make money. Sometimes they take a gamble and invest on instinct, perhaps with a bit of research to back them up. Sometimes they switch direction, depending on how things are going for them.

Planters

Over 40 per cent of the investors the regulator talked to are long-termers who like the safety of diversified funds and well-known companies and sectors with a strong future.

Planters invest as a substitute for saving, trying to make their money work harder for themselves and the economy than it would in a bank account.

Opportunists

About 20 per cent of investors are opportunists, backing their knowledge and expertise to allow them to make significant investment gains. They have a long-term focus but adjust their investments and strategies frequently and focus on building self-knowledge. Some people in this group have lots of experience while others have only just recently started.

Dabblers

Another 20 per cent of investors are controlled and cautious, using only a small proportion of their money to invest. They are usually good money managers who just want a better return on their savings. Online platforms make investing easier and more accessible for them and they're becoming more confident making their own decisions.

Making a difference to the world

Another great aspect to investing is that you can use your money to create the world you want to live in. This is a big driver for a lot of the people we see using Sharesies. They want to build wealth, but not just for themselves, and not always just financial wealth.

It sounds like a big claim, right, that you can change the world with your investments?

Well, you can. You get to choose what you think the best thing is to do with every dollar you make, and every dollar you spend, and that can mean different things to different people.

Think about it this way. If you believe strongly that chickens shouldn't live in cages, when you go to the supermarket you might deliberately seek out free-range chicken products and eggs, even if they cost you a little more. You vote with your spending for the type of products you want supermarkets to put on their shelves. Over time the more people who buy free-range chicken, the better the business performs. Sometimes this can even lower the cost of the product, too.

It's the same with investing — you choose where you put your money. If you identify a company that is delivering change that you want to see, or developing products you really believe in, investing in them should create change in the world, as well as hopefully delivering you some healthy returns. As a shareholder, you also have the ability to vote and influence the direction of the company.

While your investment fund is growing, it could also be helping a start-up get on its feet or a business make moves towards a more sustainable future. Sonya sometimes says she likes to think that while she's off living her life, or even when she's asleep, she's making an impact with her investments. They're out there creating change even while she's doing other things. That's some impressive multi-tasking!

When you have a portfolio that reflects your own values and beliefs, it drives you to be more engaged with the world and the community you live in. We reckon that can only be a good thing.

There is a catch (of course)

The reason you will generally earn a higher return from investing in shares than you do when you put your money in a bank account is that investing in shares comes with extra risk. Shares are investments in real companies that take part in the real world.

Risk largely exists because none of us have a crystal ball to see the future. It's another way of describing the level of 'uncertainty' there is about a predicted outcome.

We want to add a very important point here. 'Risk' in the context of investing doesn't mean something is necessarily bad. It just means that there are things you need to know, consider and expect, if you want higher returns on your investment. You'll also need to put in place techniques to help you manage risk. As economist and investor Benjamin Graham said, successful investing is about managing risk, not avoiding it.

Before you leap in, it's important to come to terms with the fact that investment markets don't always go up. That's not designed to scare you off — we just don't want you to get knocked off track by any surprises. Ups and downs are a normal part of how markets behave. You can achieve outstanding returns from investing in shares but you can also lose money, particularly if you don't know what to expect.

Some people are fine with the idea of their investment balances moving around a lot and they can handle seeing their balance fall every so often. But others find this really difficult and might get scared and bail out at the wrong moment, which is where the problems start.

Your investments dropping in value is not necessarily a problem. You only lock in a loss when you sell. Selling at the wrong moment can be a very expensive mistake, when hanging in there may have seen things bounce back. Selling at the wrong time is what we want to help you avoid.

Working out how much risk you are comfortable with will help guide you in finding the type of investment that might be right for you and make your investment experience more enjoyable. It's possible to find higher- and lower-risk investments, even among shares.

Generally, the younger you are (or the longer you're investing for), the more risk you may be able to take — and the reward you may get for taking that risk is that your returns may be higher because of it.

You can see this really clearly in a superannuation fund using the Sorted Retirement Calculator online: If you're 25 and in a conservative fund for your working life, earning about $60,000 now and contributing 6 per cent of that income a year, you could end up with about $205,000.

But if you were in a growth fund that might move around a bit more but has potential to deliver greater returns on average, you might get $310,000, even if you were putting the same amount aside each pay.

Here are a few questions to help you figure out what an appropriate level of risk is for you to take (and hopefully maximise your returns because of it).

What's your time horizon?

The first thing to think about is how long you want to invest for.

You can expect that markets will move over the time you are investing (more on why that happens shortly). The dips are part of what helps you make better returns, because they give you a chance to invest and ride the recovery. What matters is how much time you have to ride it out.

If you know you'll need to use the money soon, you're likely to need to take less risk because you don't know how things will look in a few months' time when you need to withdraw your funds. For example, at a time you invest in a company their share price could be at an all-time high. Does this mean they'll be higher in six months? Or lower? Or about the same?

We don't know, because we don't have a crystal ball. That's a problem if you know you want the money for a deposit on a house purchase that's settling in eight weeks.

But if you are investing with no clear end point in mind, or for a goal that is still many years away, you can afford to take a lot more risk.

What we do know is that over the long term — we're talking 15 years, 20 years or more — a well-diversified portfolio with a bit of risk should increase in value at a faster rate than you'd get from a lower-risk investment. Some reasons for this include the emergence of new technology, making businesses more productive, and more people joining in the global population of workers, consumers and business owners.

Your time horizon is the period between when you invest your money, and when you expect to need it. A short time horizon is typically within the next two or three years, while a long time horizon would be over 10 years.

If your time horizon is long, you don't have to worry about what happens in the short term. In the scheme of things, day-to-day or year-to-year fluctuations get smoothed out by the overall rising trend. You'll almost always look back on an investment from 10 years ago and wish you'd invested more back then — even if there were a few wobbles along the way.

The more risk you take, the better your potential reward or loss. The Financial Markets Authority, New Zealand's financial markets regulator, found that 14 per cent of investors in 2021 were looking for a 'moon shot' and were OK with risking a lot of money if there was a big reward — such as the opportunity to get in while shares were cheap on a company that went on to be a huge success. If you know you have the money available to take that sort of risk, that can be great.

What's your investment personality?

But consider your personality, too.

While it's true that you may get higher returns by taking on more risk, you need to also invest in a way that you're comfortable with. If you're not comfortable taking risks, you're more likely to panic and sell when your investment drops in value. This would leave you worse off than before, particularly because people who are prone to panic seem to sell at the low point, and then not get back in until things have recovered significantly.

If you know you're the anxious type, are there any steps you could take now to help yourself deal with uncomfortable market movements in the future? It might help to make a note in your phone to remind yourself that you were expecting some downs as well as ups, stick a bookmark in this chapter or add a Post-it to your computer screen.

Still not sure how much risk you should take?

As well as thinking about your investment horizon and your personality, you could also take into account the following questions:

- Do you have other money available to you? If you have a good income and other savings available to you, you can afford to take more risk.
- Do you have a lot of debt?
- How secure is your job?
- How do you feel about the idea of losing money? If you feel like you could cope with the idea that it's just part of investing, dial it up. You'll probably do better in the long run.

Is it ever too late to get started?

We don't mean to give the impression that investing in shares is only for younger people, or that if you're a bit older you can't afford to take the risks that could deliver great returns.

The truth is, no matter how old you are, you can reap benefits from investing.

We know that everyone's situation is different. But on average, people tend to earn more money in their forties and fifties than they did in their twenties.

When you're in your forties, you've had 20 more years of building your skills and qualifications. You might also have more savings, or a successful business. It makes sense that a 45-year-old would have (on average) $500 more to spend each week than a 25-year-old. Don't be put off if you're starting to invest later in life — your higher earning power means you may be able to catch up to your 25-year-old self more quickly than you think. The best time to start investing is now.

Ultimately, if you have more money in your pocket than you did when you were 25, this means you can invest more than you could have back then, while continuing to enjoy your lifestyle.

No matter your age, your time horizon might turn out to be longer than you think. It's easy to think that younger people have longer time horizons, and older people have shorter time horizons. But the truth is more complicated than that.

For one, remember that life is long (hopefully). If you're 45, and you're investing for your retirement at age 65, you still have 20 years to go. If you intend on working longer than that, you have even more than 20 years. Twenty years is a really long time horizon. You can put that time to work by investing in a higher-risk, diversified set of assets that should give you a solid long-term return.

If you look at your financial goals, and find that you have a fairly long time horizon, you may be able to have the best of both worlds as an 'older' investor. Not only can you invest in higher-risk, higher-return investments, you also have more money to invest because your income is better.

There are all kinds of investment options in between very low-risk savings, and higher-risk, high-return investing. You can spread your money around different investments that suit your specific time horizon, slicing and dicing your investments any way you want and tailoring your portfolio to your investment goals by spreading your money across a bunch of different levels and kinds of risk and return.

Why do markets move?

Investment markets aren't mysterious machines that operate independently from the real world. Markets move because of things that are happening in the world — things which you may be able to see going on all around you.

Investor confidence is a big factor that affects share prices as a whole. If people are feeling good about the future, they're likely to be willing to pay more for shares in companies that they see as likely to benefit from that positive future. But if they're worried about the future — for example, if there's been a run of bad news like higher unemployment, increasing inflation or something out of left field like a pandemic — prices can fall because people worry that the outlook is not so rosy.

Things that happen and move a market as a whole are sometimes referred to as systemic risks — they affect the whole economy, and there's not a lot you can do to avoid them. But knowing what's going on, and understanding that it's just part of investing, can help you to spot opportunities rather than worry too much.

There are also factors that can cause an individual company's share price to move. A company might have a new market or product that people are excited about, which pushes its share price up, or it might have a new competitor that makes it less appealing to investors. For example, Blockbuster, an American company that rented videos and DVDs, was doing great in the 1990s. But Blockbuster no longer exists today, thanks to competitors like

Netflix (NASDAQ:NFLX). Blockbuster continued to rent videos and DVDs when customers wanted streaming services — and now, partly because of that, Blockbuster is gone. In these situations you'll need to think about whether what's happening is a short-term thing or a death blow.

Ways to invest

There are two main ways that you can get a slice of the equities action. (Equities is another word for stocks and shares.)

You can buy shares in specific companies, which gives you a small slice of the ownership of that specific business, or you can put your money into a fund that invests it in a whole basket of stuff, including shares, bonds, property and other assets.

Direct investments in shares tend to be higher risk because you are directly exposed to the fortunes of one company. You literally become a part-owner and get all the benefits and problems that come with that. So if you invest in a company that is on a strong growth trajectory, as a direct investor you're primed to get a slice of that.

In terms of funds, there are options available to fit a range of risk profiles and areas that investors might be interested in — from ultra-growth funds chasing big gains by investing in shares in growing companies, to some that dial back the risk with investments in bonds or even cash. Some funds passively ride a market index and others actively choose what they carry.

Funds offer more diversification because your money is immediately spread between different investments, which also spreads your risk. This can be helpful if you don't have a lot of money to invest, because it is harder to effectively diversify small amounts yourself. Twenty dollars in a fund gives you a lot more diversification than five dollars in four companies.

You can spread your investment across as many different funds and companies as you choose, selecting investments that align with your investing vision, and your view of where the world could be headed and which businesses are well placed to ride that wave.

Each investment is part of your overall portfolio and your investment plan. Think about the bigger picture as you add investments to your portfolio.

If you make investments you're comfortable with, you're going to be more likely to stick with investing. And the more you invest, the more comfortable you'll become with the movements of the market, which means you might then invest in more risky and potentially higher-returning investments later.

What's a bond?

A bond is basically a loan. When you buy bonds — either from a company or a government — you're giving that money in return for interest payments from the borrower. You'll get the money back at a set end date, or you can on-sell the bond before that date. If the bond is delivering higher interest payments than the market offers, the value of the bond to a prospective purchaser will rise. If the interest payments are lower, its value will fall.

Keep checking in

It's tempting to set and forget, but you don't want to totally ignore your investments once you've set them up.

As you become more comfortable with investing, your

tolerance for risk may increase (or decrease). Your income may change, or you may decide to change your spending habits. There may be some changes or external factors affecting the market. All these things flow into your decisions about the amount you invest and what you invest in.

Set yourself a reminder to check in every few months. Are your investments still a good fit for you, or could you afford to be investing a bit more? What are your goals, and are you on track?

Sometimes having a friend who is on a similar investment path can help — check in with each other, and hold each other accountable to remain on track.

Starting from scratch

If you currently have no savings whatsoever, you might want to consider building up an emergency fund at the same time as your other investments that you can have quick access to. Some financial advisors often suggest having an amount set aside that is equal to about three months' pay.

The amount you need will depend a lot on your circumstances, but it's helpful to have some backup in case something goes wrong with your car, or you have to move house unexpectedly, or your dog eats a sock and has to have emergency surgery.

You probably don't want to build up your emergency fund in a sharemarket investment because the market might be having an off-day on the same day your dog has its expedition through your laundry. Investments aren't as quick to access as cash in the bank. But you could consider building your emergency fund by investing in conservative funds if that meets your needs. These funds are a good way to reduce your risk — you could even choose a cash fund, which invests in cash and cash equivalents like deposits and short-term debt securities from banks and big businesses.

Can investing in shares make up for not having a house?

Our relationship with home ownership is changing, and it's complicated. We often think of owning a home through a financial and investing lens, but this isn't the only reason people want to buy their own house (stability, painting the walls, renovating) or not (ongoing maintenance). Like anything, personal preference drives decision making.

Regardless of the drivers, for lots of young people the prospect of home ownership is looking further and further away — if it's even going to be achievable at all.

The way governments around the world responded to Covid-19 pushed up asset prices (like houses). That's created more of a gap between the asset owners and those with all their wealth in cash.

If you're part of 'generation rent', you might wonder how to achieve financial stability when the traditional method — owning and paying off a house or two — is out of reach, at least for now.

The good news is, shares and other investments can be a big part of a wealth journey even if you don't own a home.

The big difference between home ownership and shares is leverage. While you can have 10 per cent or 20 per cent of the value of a house as a deposit, and borrow the rest to get into your first home, usually with shares you only invest what you have to contribute.

That means you are less exposed to the gains — someone with a 20 per cent deposit on a $1 million house will double their money when the house increases in value by 20 per cent. Someone who invests $200,000 in shares that make a 20 per cent return only gets the 20 per cent.

But investing in shares is a good way to ensure that your savings keep pace with the property market. A big problem for many would-be homeowners is that the deposit they require increases more quickly than their savings increase. If you're investing in shares you get access to potentially higher returns than what is available if that money was just in the bank.

You can also invest with any amount and start whenever you like, depending on the provider you choose to invest with.

You can also get exposure to the property market through listed companies and funds that invest in residential and commercial property and can build your wealth over time.

The most important thing is to keep building your assets and make decisions that align to your goals.

What you can do now to get started

- Work out how much you want to invest to start you off. Remember, it's totally fine to start with a small amount while you learn how everything works and build up from there. Your $1 will go on the same journey as $1000 and will deliver all the same investment lessons (which also are a huge investment in your future).
- Pick the investments you want to start with. What companies do you connect with? Which funds sound like they're backing your interests? Don't get too technical at this stage. You're only getting started. Give yourself space to learn.

- Start watching your investment do its thing. Don't feel that you have to be obsessive about checking your portfolio value every day — it can be fun to keep an eye out for things happening in the world that will affect the value of your investment but you don't have to fret about every share price movement. After all, if you own your own home you don't come home at the end of the day and check your letterbox to see whether the value of your house has gone up or down. Your portfolio may grow over time and it's not something to be constantly worrying about. You've probably got enough to worry about already!

Six surprise benefits of investing

- It makes you feel as though your money is on your side and might turn around a previously negative relationship with your finances.
- You can help to make the changes you want to see in the world.
- Being young is a massive benefit — having time on your side means you can get the benefit of more years of returns without a lot of money to invest.
- It'll give you a reason to engage with the news — is what's happening in the world benefitting the companies you're investing in?
- You can monitor trends — but not so you can go shopping for an on-point outfit. Instead, use that knowledge to pick trends that could make a company a great investment.
- You'll discover that you, and your ability to earn and learn, are your biggest asset.

Did you know?

- In 2016, a Financial Markets Authority study reported that 56 per cent of New Zealanders said they were confident in the financial markets[7] — but those who were confident were more likely to be male Aucklanders, living with a partner and no kids and earning more than $100,000 as a household. Those who were not confident were more likely to be aged 18 to 29, female, single and earning a lower income.
- Two thirds of people had invested in KiwiSaver.
- Just 21 per cent owned shares they had bought themselves, and 11 per cent were invested in managed funds.
- In 2021 that same research showed that 72 per cent of New Zealanders were confident in the financial markets, and six out of every 10 people who had bought shares themselves had used an online platform like Sharesies. People who used an online platform to buy their shares were significantly more likely to be aged between 25 to 39 years. Things are moving in the right direction!

---

7 'Investor confidence report – annual results', FMA (website), https://www.fma.govt.nz/news-and-resources/reports-and-papers/investor-confidence-report-annual-results/

3.

What to invest in

You're on your way. You've set some goals and started putting some money aside to start achieving that financial future you've been dreaming about.

Now you get to the fun bit — deciding what to invest in.

The possibilities for potential investments are almost endless. We'll focus on funds and shares because that's what we deal with every day.

What makes a good investment?

The definition of a 'good investment' can be quite subjective but very broadly, it is usually something that grows in value over time, and perhaps delivers a good stream of income while it's doing that — and maybe does some good in the world around you.

You might invest in shares in a start-up company you believe in and hope to see it increase in value over the years, for example. Or you might buy shares in a really reliable infrastructure company that may give you a better return in dividends than you could get from the bank.

Although none of us have a crystal ball, the difference between a lucky guess and a good investment is that you understand the fundamentals of what you're putting your money into, and what's driving the future value you're expecting.

Here's the 101 on what you need to know as you get ready to dive in a bit deeper and get excited about your investing future.

Shares

First up, shares.

When you buy a share you're literally buying a small piece of the company. Most new investors take a very small slice of a very big company. By buying shares, you can own a bit of anything from ANZ Bank (Australia and New Zealand Banking Group NZX:ASX:ANZ) to Amazon (Amazon.com Inc. NASDAQ:AMZN), Roblox (Roblox Corporation NYSE:RBLX) to Facebook (now Meta Platforms Inc. NASDAQ:META). You can buy shares in companies in your own country, or in other countries around the world.

You can't just rock up to any company you like and ask to buy some shares (well not yet, anyway). When companies are willing to take investments from the public, they list on a stock exchange (administered by the NZX in New Zealand and ASX in Australia). When companies are trading on the stock exchange they are described as publicly listed and anyone with a bit of cash to invest can get in on the action, if they want to. These listed companies also have obligations to disclose information that's relevant to shareholders and people who might consider buying shares, such as how much money they are making or any big changes in strategy.

In contrast, if you're investing in a private company (one that's not available to be bought or sold on an exchange), it's up to its current owners to decide who gets to own shares and how much information they'd like to share with them.

You usually make money from investing in shares in two ways: through dividends, which are paid during the time you are holding the stock, and any capital gain when you decide to sell your shares.

Dividends

Owning shares gives you a right to a portion of the profits of the company when they are paid out as dividends or distributions to shareholders.

The amount you get depends on the size of your shareholding. You'll usually see this reported as an amount per share when a company announces its financial results. For example, in the year to 30 June 2020, ASB (NZX:ABB) (that's the New Zealand arm of Commonwealth Bank of Australia ASX:CBA) paid dividends of 65.07 cents per share. So, if you owned 1000 shares, you'd have been paid dividends of $650.70.

Dividends are not guaranteed. Sometimes a company will decide not to pay a dividend in a particular year, sometimes because it has not delivered a profit or it decides to invest it back into the business for growth.

While dividends can give a regular flow of income from your shares, people also invest with the aim of capital gains. (Yes, like you hear about in the property market.)

Capital gains

You make a capital gain when you sell a share for more than you bought it for. The 'profit' is called a capital gain.

For example, in March 2020, Westpac (ASX:NZX:WBC) shares were trading for just under $15 on the ASX. In March 2021, they were about $25. If you'd bought in 2020 and sold in 2021, the $10 you made per share would be referred to as the capital gain.

The important difference between dividends and capital gains is that capital gains can go backwards. It's possible for shares to drop in value, so you won't always receive a capital gain — although the longer you hold the shares, the more likely a capital gain becomes.

Your rights as a shareholder

While being a small-scale shareholder will not give you the ability to storm the boardroom and demand everyone follows your new business plan, it does give you some rights.

Often if you own a full share in a company, you're able to vote at the company's annual general meeting. Your one vote might not sound very much but if you band together with other shareholders, you can become a real force to encourage change. There are lots of organisations and individuals who do exactly this — they get together, and use their ownership power to force companies to alter their behaviour. This is sometimes a strategy used by people who want to improve things like the way a business treats workers or the environment — it's called 'impact investing' and we'll get into that a bit later on.

As a shareholder, you're also entitled to regular updates and information about what is going on at the company.

The $1 million question: What sort of shares are a winner?

There is a wide range of businesses listed on the sharemarket, from the big businesses everyone has heard of like power companies, airports, airlines and banks through to relatively new start-up businesses.

When you're deciding what to buy, it can help to get out your crystal ball.

What do you think the world will be like in 10 years' time? Will that be a good environment for the company you're thinking of buying shares in, or is its moment likely to have passed? Take Zoom (NASDAQ:ZM) for example. Did Covid-19 give it its moment, and will it be overtaken by something else — or has the world changed in such a way that Zoom's outlook is much brighter? What would need to happen for the business to succeed, or to fail?

You can sometimes get some inspiration by looking at what your friends, workmates and neighbours are up to. We spoke to a fund manager who invested in Giant Bicycles (TPE:9921) after noticing how many people were buying and riding bikes through the lockdown.

Through the Covid-19 lockdown experience we saw some trends really come to the fore — as well as those virtual catchups that helped propel Zoom's share price during the pandemic, all of a sudden it seemed that more people were into golf, e-bikes and getting a dog.

With your investor hat on, you can look at what is going on in the world and think about what that might mean for your investment opportunities. If you see lots of people you know buying a certain food for breakfast on the way to work, you don't have to set up your own food business to make the most of the trend — you could invest in someone else's company that is already doing it.

If everyone is getting into a particular trend, what industry does that benefit, and which companies could have the edge? Importantly, is it a passing fad or an actual shift in demand that should improve a company's fortunes over time?

Use this as a chance to 'get hypothesising' and wonder about the future. When you imagine the world of a few years' time, what are people into, what do they care about? How do they spend their time and where do they spend their money?

Think about what you know

When you're getting started, it can be a good idea to invest in companies that you are familiar with, and in industries that interest you. That makes it a lot more 'engaging' to keep up with what's going on with your investments because they are things you would want to read about anyway.

Lots of people can think of companies that they really like and go out of their way to support and buy from. Just as many (if not more) people have companies that they really don't like. Maybe you can think of a company that's doing great work every year and developing better and better products, but you're still mad at another company for the way they handled your customer service inquiry, or you're worried about the environmental effects of something that it's doing.

Either way, if you love a company and want to see it go from strength to strength in the future, you can send that message by investing in it. And if a company's values don't align with yours, you can take a personal stand by not adding it to your portfolio.

New Zealand and Australian investors tend to have a strong

home bias, investing in companies in their own countries, as well as an interest in United States stocks. Those are the markets we're most familiar with.

There are sound reasons why investing locally, and in what you know, makes sense.

If you invest close to home, you might know people who work in a business, or be more familiar with the environment the company is working in and what could impact its success. Some people suggest that you shouldn't invest too heavily in the industry you work in because if something were to happen that negatively affected it, you could find your investments take a hit at the same time as your job gets a bit wobbly. More on this when we get to diversification soon.

Investor story: Building a savings habit

Sally joined Sharesies when it was still in the beta stage and says it has really helped her build savings habits. She took a large amount of money out when she bought her first home but has since started to see it grow again.

Control

One of the main reasons that people invest directly in shares is that it's a really hands-on experience that puts you in control of exactly what is in your portfolio. You aren't relying on a fund manager to pick the stocks they think will be a good fit — it's all down to you, your research and your view of the future deciding on the best place to put your money.

You can create the exact portfolio that matches your risk tolerance, preferences and values. If you had $100 to invest, you could put $1 in each of 100 companies, $2 in each of 50 companies, $90 in one company and $1 in each of 10 other companies, and so on — it's completely up to you.

You might feel really strongly about the opportunities ahead for one company and put all your money into its shares and nothing else. This can be a risky move, because it may not perform as you expected. Of course, if it does as well, or better than, you hoped, you'll end up pretty happy.

Or you might be on the other end of the spectrum. You can invest in a broad range of shares through an exchange-traded fund (ETF) that meets your circumstances and strategy, without needing to invest in them individually. And each ETF has its own purpose. For example, the Smartshares NZ Top 50 Fund (FNZ), available on the NZX, enables its investors to invest in the 50 largest companies listed on the NZX, without needing to invest directly into them. However, you might find that some shares in an ETF don't align with your strategy or values, therefore, you might gravitate more towards selecting your own companies and investing in them separately, so you can have greater control of which companies you're supporting.

If you're a more advanced investor, you can use this flexibility and control to test new strategies. For example, you could do some research and find some companies that you think are going to perform really well in the future. Then you can put your money where your mouth is by investing in them. If your investment does better than an index like the NZ Top 50, then great work. Your strategy met your objectives — and you probably learned something along the way as well. If it doesn't — you've learned this might not be the strategy for you.

Many investors have a mix of funds and shares. You can add some investments in companies to ETF and managed fund investments, and more precisely direct your money towards the outcome you want — whether that's a financial outcome for yourself, an outcome for a company, or an outcome for society in general. Your goals and how you get there are up to you — investing in companies is just another tool to help make it happen.

Another benefit of direct share investing is that you'll only pay the cost of the share transaction — there is no ongoing fee charged by a manager looking after the investment.

Who decides the share price?

The market is where investors come together to buy or sell shares — for example, the New Zealand stock exchange (NZX), Australian stock exchange (ASX) or New York Stock Exchange (NYSE). When you place an order for a company or ETF, it goes 'on market'.

If you want to buy shares, you tell the exchange how many you want to buy, and the most you're willing to pay for them. If you want to sell shares, you tell the exchange how many you want to sell, and the lowest amount you'll accept for them. So, if you say you're willing to sell some shares for as low as $10 per share, and someone else is willing to buy shares for as high as $12, they could end up buying your shares for $10. This process happens over and over again, throughout the day.

On one side of the market, you have the buyers with their bids (the highest amount they're willing to pay per share), and on the other side, you have the sellers with their offers (the lowest amount they're willing to accept per share). This line-up of buyers and sellers is called the market depth.

Let's look at an example.

On the buyer side, you have someone willing to buy 700 shares at no more than \$2.55 per share. On the seller side, you have someone wanting to sell 150 of their shares at no less than \$2.58 per share. The difference between what buyers are willing to pay and what sellers are willing to accept at any given time on the market is called the spread.

A trade occurs when a buyer and seller match on a price. This happens when either the seller lowers their offer to meet a buyer's bid, or when the buyer increases their bid to meet a seller's offer.

You can see the last traded price on the stock exchange websites but the price you buy and sell at could well be different from what you see displayed. The last traded price changes every time someone buys or sells a particular share. There is a threshold for what size trade will alter the price. Some smaller trades won't alter it. A trade that is big enough to change the last traded price is called a price-setting trade.

There are two types of orders:

Market orders

Market orders are typically used when investors want an order to be processed quickly and are willing to let the market decide the price. When Sharesies places your order on the market, we check to see if there's a buyer or seller at (or near) the last traded price for that share. If not, we try to get you the best available price, without causing any issues in the market. To do this, we look at things like the last traded price, market conditions, and availability of buyers or sellers. We make adjustments until we find a price to trade at within a limit that we set.

Limit orders

Limit orders give you more control to buy or sell shares at a specific price. When you place a buy limit order, you can set a maximum price that you're willing to pay for a share. When you place a sell limit order, you can set the minimum price that you're willing to sell at.

Managed funds, ETFs, shares: what's the difference?

If you don't want to pick your investments yourself, or you want an easy way to spread your investment across a range of things, you can opt to invest in a fund. Instead of owning shares in one company, funds are like a basket of companies.

Funds take your money, and that of other investors, and pool it together to make investments.

Every fund has a strategy that determines the sorts of things that it will invest in, the risk it will take and the fees it will charge.

Some funds invest in cash, some in property, some in bonds, some in shares — and most in a mix of all sorts of assets to deliver the sorts of outcomes that their investors are looking for. Once you've made an investment, you can leave the worrying about exactly where the money is going to the fund manager, which some people find a reassuring prospect.

Exchange-traded funds

ETFs have become really popular in recent years. One of the reasons is that they often are index funds that simply track an index (remember those?) and mirror its returns, which can be a cheaper method of investing and — some say — just as effective as trying to pick winners through active management.

While fund managers individually pick each company, an exchange-traded fund follows a set of rules that drive the investment selection. For example, the Smartshares Australian Top 20 ETF (OZY) holds shares in the top 20 companies in Australia.

As the name suggests, exchange-traded funds are funds that have their units trade on a stock exchange.

Overall, exchange-traded funds tend to be more targeted to specific types of investments than other managed funds, for example focusing only on New Zealand's top 50 listed companies (FNZ), Healthcare Innovation (LIV), or Emerging Markets (EMG).

You can use index funds to diversify your portfolio and invest passively. But not every index fund is created equal. Some that sound as though they should be quite similar can end up delivering quite different returns. You can get lots of information on any index fund you're considering, compare it against your goals and values, then make a decision about what to invest in and how much to invest.

Active vs passive funds

Funds are usually described as active or passive (although sometimes people will try to roll out terms like 'actively passive' just to confuse you!)

Active management is when a fund manager is constantly checking on an investment and actively selecting the things that are in the fund. They'll try to beat a market's returns, doing better than everyone else when things are good and limiting losses when they're not. Spoiler — this isn't easy and they don't always get it right.

Passive management means that the fund manager doesn't actively select what is in the fund. They just mirror a market index and their investors' returns mirror whatever the market is doing at that time.

An index fund won't always track its index perfectly

Sometimes the investments within an index change. Take that Smartshares NZ Top 50 ETF (FNZ) we mentioned just now — if a new company entered the top 50 and another one left, the fund would have to sell out of one and buy into another. This process is called a rebalance. You'd see it happening in any index fund that pledged to hold a certain mix of investments.

If there are no sellers for a share the index fund wants to buy, or no buyers for a share the index fund wants to sell, the composition of shares it owns could end up differing from the index it's tracking for a while. This will make the fund's returns different from that of the index.

Index fund managers also charge fees to cover their costs and to make a profit. These fees can vary a lot between different fund managers — even though they might be tracking the same index. These differences in fees can impact your returns. Checking out a fund you're thinking about before you invest can help you to compare what managers charge and what you're getting for that money.

An index fund might apply additional weighting to shares in its portfolio that means returns are slightly different from the returns of the index it tracks.

For example, the Smartshares NZ Top 50 ETF (FNZ) applies weighting so that it never invests more than 5 per cent of the fund's total in any one company. This means it provides more equal exposure to the companies in the index, even though it's not tracking the index precisely. If a really big company was outperforming the rest of the top 50, you might not see the same effect in the fund.

Managed funds

A managed fund is a broader term to describe any fund under the control of a fund manager. You invest directly in the managed fund via the fund manager rather than through an exchange.

Managed funds can be actively or passively managed. The industry in general has noticed a big increase in demand from people wanting managed funds that responsibly invest their money.

You can choose a managed fund that fits your investment philosophy. Some people like the idea of leaving their investments up to the experts, which is what putting your money in an actively managed fund achieves.

Investing in managed funds is sometimes less liquid than an ETF because there is sometimes a minimum hold period. After that hold period, you can usually get your money back with a couple of days' notice.

In New Zealand, all funds and ETFs offer a product disclosure statement, and in Australia each ETF is likely to have a Target Market Determination fact sheet that you should check out before you invest your money. The product disclosure statement explains what the fund invests in, why it invests in those shares, and for what sort of investor the fund would be a good fit.

Funds will describe themselves according to the sort of risk appetite that they suit. You'll often hear them talk about being conservative, which is good for people who might want their money back within a relatively short period of time, or growth-oriented, aggressive options for people who are investing for a longer time horizon and want to supercharge their returns.

Diversification

Now we get to an important aspect of investing that we've hinted at a couple of times already: diversification.

Simply, diversification means not putting all your eggs in one basket in case that basket turns out to be not such a great investment. It's a technique used to manage the risk of investing.

To diversify, you'll need to rid yourself of the idea that you have to pick a winner with your investments — what you really want to pick is a nicely rounded portfolio that delivers the goals you're working towards, while maximising your opportunities and minimising your risks.

We like to illustrate this point with the help of Super Chicken.

Say you've got $100, and you want to get into the egg business (free range of course). Luckily for you, a chicken salesman has a Super Chicken that he'll sell you for $100.

Super Chicken can lay 10 eggs a week, and you can sell them for $1 each. It's a no-brainer, right? You'll make your money back in 10 weeks, and on week 11, you'll be making pure profit. You'll be the egg king of your town in no time. People will come from far and wide whenever they're hungry for an omelette.

Unless Super Chicken gets sick and can't lay eggs for a while. Or the neighbour's cat gets too close. Maybe Super Chicken goes way too free range and starts laying her eggs all over the garden, and you can't find them.

If any of these things happen, what's your fallback? You don't have one, because you spent all your money on Super Chicken.

Here's an alternative: You buy four regular chickens for $25 each. Each chicken lays two eggs a week. Pretty solid, but hardly Super Chicken material. And you make a bit less money per week, because where Super Chicken was earning you $10 a week, these four chickens (bless them) are only making you $8 a week.

But think about the scenarios we ran through up above. If one chicken gets sick for a week, you still get $6 from the other three chickens' eggs. If that cat comes back, you've still got $4 a week to play with. And if you're having a really bad week, and the third chicken goes rogue and starts hiding eggs, you've still got $2 left over.

It's not the $8 you expected, but it's more than $0 — and three bad things have happened. With Super Chicken, if just one bad thing had happened, you would have lost your entire income.

What's the catch?

That was a lot of numbers just then, so you may have missed that Super Chicken was giving you $10 a week while the regular chickens were only giving you $8 a week. That's the price you pay for diversification. When you diversify, you sacrifice some of the profits in order to protect yourself from the losses.

The same concept applies to shares. It's not unheard of for companies to go under. If this happens and you have all your money in one company, you've just lost all your money.

There are a few ways to diversify:

Global diversification

One way to spread your risk is to diversify across countries. People often have a home bias, wanting to invest where they live. But if you earn your day-to-day income in a particular country, it might make sense to put your investments somewhere else — so if the economy hits a rough patch at home, there's a chance that your investments will still be going strong everywhere else. If your job, house and investments are all in Australia, for example, and something comes along and causes havoc there, you could see the value of everything you own fall at the same time as your employment looks shaky. But if you had investments offshore, they might still give you something to fall back on.

Diversification across industries

Downturns (and recoveries) don't tend to hit all industries equally. Think about Covid-19 — the industries that really suffered were the sectors that relied on easy international travel and open borders. Other industries did even better than they normally would during the pandemic. Having investments in companies in a few different industries means you're less likely to see the value of all your investments fall in one go.

Diversification through different investment types

You can also spread your risk by investing in a few different types of assets. A bond fund is likely to experience market movements very differently from one that's invested solely in shares.

Spreading your investment around is a better way to succeed long-term. Funds can be an easy way to do this — you can pick a few ETFs that invest in different industries, maybe, or one that invests in a range of companies from a particular country, like the Smartshares NZ Top 50 ETF (FNZ) we've talked about a few times in this chapter. Because funds are combining your money with that of other investors, they have a bigger pot of money to spread between a wider range of investments.

How to read a company's annual report

If you're thinking about buying shares in a company, you'll probably want to get as much information as you can about the company first.

One way to get a sense of how the company is going is to check out its annual report.

Companies need to share a load of information with shareholders and potential shareholders — it's part of the deal when listing on an exchange. They have to let shareholders in on all the material information that might affect the value of their shares. If they're found to have concealed information, or to have given it to only a few people, there are serious consequences.

One way they make sure all the information is made available is by releasing half-year and annual reports.

Annual reports are really handy for investors because they offer a detailed review of how the year went for a company. They have lots of information you can use for your research (also called due diligence), like how much money the company made, the business's strategy for the future, and who's on the executive team. They're also a way for you to follow the performance of companies you've already invested in.

You can generally find a company's annual report in two places:

1. On the company's website — usually in a section called something like 'investors', 'investor centre', or 'investor relations'.
2. On an exchange's website (like the New Zealand stock exchange) — usually from the company's page, where all the announcements are listed.

There are four main things you'll want to look for when you're reading through an annual report: the numbers, the strategy, the risks and the team.

The numbers

There are a few notable numbers to look out for in financial statements. These include the raw details of the business — how much money it made, how much money it spent, what it owes and how many assets it owns.

Profit

The income statements show you how much money the company made (revenue) and how much it spent (expenses) — and what it spent that money on. The difference between revenue and expenses is profit.

Profit matters more than revenue. A company may have relatively low revenue of $1 million a year, but also expenses of only $100,000 a year. That's a $900,000 profit. Not bad.

At the other end of the spectrum, a company may have revenue of $1 billion a year, but expenses of $1.5 billion a year. Even though it has enormous levels of revenue, it's actually running at a loss.

You can also check out the company's earnings per share for a quick health check. That's the total profit made, divided by the number of shares issued.

This can be an important figure to look at because it really gets to the nitty-gritty of how profitable a company is.

Of course, not all companies are profitable. That's not always a bad thing. Some companies deliberately choose to spend money on funding growth instead of profit and can make big losses on their way to later success. If that's the case for a company you're looking at, you'll want to understand why a loss is being made and what the strategy is to turn it around — and how quickly that will happen.

Price-to-earnings ratio (P/E ratio)

Have a look at the company's price-to-earnings ratio. This is the share price divided by the earnings per share.

The P/E ratio is important because it shows how much you're paying for each dollar of the company's income. A company may have high earnings per share, but a low P/E ratio, because the company's share price is also quite low.

For example, if a company has earnings of $30 million, and 10 million shares outstanding, the company's earnings per share would be $3 per share. If the company's share price was $60, the company's P/E ratio would be 20.

Dividends

You might also want to look at a company's dividend yield. This is important because it's part of what you get in return for your investment.

Dividend yield is the percentage of the share price that the company has paid out in dividends in the past year. This is helpful in estimating what kind of return on your investment you might get.

So, if a company's shares were $1 each, and it paid 10 cents per share in dividends last year, then its dividend yield would be 10 per cent. If the shares were $2 each, and it paid 10 cents per share, its dividend yield would be 5 per cent.

In this way, dividend yield is similar to the P/E ratio, in that the yield changes if the share price changes. The dividend yield can go down, even if the dividend doesn't change, if the share price goes up. The reverse can happen as well.

It's important to note that what a company decided to pay in dividends in the past may be quite different to what it will do in the future.

Equity

Companies are basically built out of two main building blocks: assets and liabilities. An asset is something the company owns that has value, like a machine, land or a brand. A liability is a debt owed by the company — like a bank loan, some existing bonds, or even money promised to employees and suppliers.

A company's equity is its total assets minus its total liabilities.

A good way to think of this is to compare it to your personal finances. If you had $10,000 in the bank, but had a personal loan of $20,000, your total equity would be negative $10,000. On the other hand, if you had $5000 in the bank, and no debt at all, your total equity would be $5000.

But like everything, equity isn't the whole picture. Think of your personal finances again: you might have $10,000 in the bank, and a $30,000 student loan. However, a government student loan has some pretty attractive terms — no, or comparatively low, interest to a bank loan and repayments based on your income. So, while the equity situation might be a bit dire at the moment, it may also pay off in the future as you pay down the loan and enjoy higher earning power from your education.

It's the same with companies — some companies may have low equity at the moment, because they're investing towards growing in the future. When you're thinking about investing, consider the debt the company is carrying and why. Does it make sense in terms of the company's overall strategy?

Return on equity

Equity is essentially the total amount of money a company has invested. You can use a company's earnings to calculate its return on equity. If a company's equity is $100 million, and it made $10 million in earnings this year, then its return on equity is 10 per cent.

This is a really useful tool, because you can compare a company's return on equity to what it could have made by investing elsewhere. For example, think about a situation where term deposit rates are around 3 per cent. If a company has a return on equity of less than 3 per cent, you might wonder why it bothered — it could have sold its assets, put the money in the bank, and made a better return on equity. Of course, it could just be going through a rough patch, or investing in future growth, but it's worth figuring out the return on equity in order to ask these questions.

Earnings before interest, tax, depreciation and amortisation (EBITDA)

This one looks complicated, but it really isn't. Earnings are pretty straightforward — they're the revenue a company has made, minus its expenses. However, lots of people prefer EBITDA because it strips out some things that can be distracting.

For example, let's say you had two companies. One made $1 million in profit by selling things to its customers. The other made $1 million in profit by selling $800,000 worth of things to its customers, and another $200,000 in interest income by putting a spare $6.6 million in a term deposit with a 3 per cent interest rate for a year.

If you just looked at net profit, these two companies would look the same. But if you looked at the EBITDA of these companies, the first one would have $1 million profit, while the second would have $800,000. EBITDA helps to remove all these other sources of income and expenses, and gives you a clear view of what the business is actually capable of producing. After all, anyone with money can put it in a term deposit — it's much more impressive for a company to make money by actually making things and selling them to people.

The downside of EBITDA is that it can hide expenses. For example, if you had a company that owned a factory that needed to be replaced every 20 years, you would see one twentieth of that factory's value as an expense on its annual report every year — this is called depreciation.

The EBITDA figure removes this expense, which may make the company look more valuable than it is. After all, the company still owns the factory, needs to maintain it, and will need to replace it someday. So, like everything, understand what you're looking at when you look at EBITDA. It has some strengths, but it also has weaknesses.

It's about the mix

These are a few terms you might run into when you're reading up on companies to invest in. The key thing to remember is that none of these terms gives you a perfect view of a company, and they can't tell you whether the company is worth investing in. But when you understand what these terms are telling you, and compare them against each other, you can use them to think about your investing approach, goals, time horizon and whether the investment is a good fit for you.

And remember, there are other ways to choose what companies to invest in. Some investors invest without looking at any figures like this at all. People invest in companies they want to see succeed, or companies they enjoy doing business with, or companies whose values are in line with theirs — you can invest based on any criteria you want. You might just decide you like the chief executive and want to get involved with what that person is doing. The actual decision about where you put your money is completely up to you — only you can decide the criteria that make something a great investment for you.

Strategy

You can find the company's overall strategy in the letters from the chief executive and chair at the beginning of the annual report. If you want more detail, you can look at the investor presentation, which is a separate document that usually comes out around the same time as the annual report.

Strategy is important because it tells you what the company plans to do in the future, and the trade-offs it'll make to get there. But keep in mind that some of these presentations will take a very optimistic view of the world, so it still pays to go through the details and check it all stacks up.

The strategy will include things like how fast the company wants to grow. Some companies might invest in fast growth at the expense of profit, and this can continue for many years. This means less profit today, in exchange for a shot at much higher profits in the future.

Other companies might slowly and steadily grow, making higher profit in the short term, while sacrificing the opportunity to grow as quickly as they could have. Most companies will fall somewhere in between these two extremes.

While some companies grow faster than others, almost all companies grow to some extent. Will the one you are looking at be expanding into new markets? Will it be finding ways to sell more things to existing customers? Will it be acquiring new businesses?

Managing costs is another key part of a company's strategy. Most companies look for ways to keep their costs down as they grow, and make sure they're spending money on the right things.

Look at how a company plans on doing this. Will it be restructuring? Outsourcing some things? Investing in new technologies?

When you are buying shares you are investing in a company's future. For that reason, it's useful to know how the company plans on getting there.

Alongside the strategy for the future, you'll also find an update on what's happened in the past. It's useful to compare this to earlier reports, and see how well it matches up. Does this company have a track record of doing what it says it'll do? If not, what stopped it from doing so?

The risks

The other side of the strategy is the risks the company faces. You'll also find these in those chair and chief executive letters at the start of the annual report.

Risks are a good counterbalance to strategy because strategy shows where the company sees itself in the future. The risks give you an idea of what kind of things may stop it from getting there. These two pieces of information can help you with your due diligence.

The team

Finally, it's useful to look at who's in charge. Company reports tell you who is on the board, and who the top executives are. These people are ultimately in charge of the company's direction, and with it your investment — so take a look at their bios in the annual report. Go ahead and google them, too. You might find a TED talk that gives you a sense of a person.

It's useful to do this after you read about the strategy and risks. Once you have your head around the strategy, you can ask yourself if the management and governance teams have the skills to execute it.

Finally, you may want to ask yourself if the backgrounds of the management team are consistent with your values.

Corporate reports can be long and hard to decipher if you try to read them from front to back. By just focusing on a few key things — the numbers, the strategy, the risks and the team — it's a lot easier to get a general picture of the company. This information should help you make clearer investment decisions, without getting overwhelmed.

IPOs: What are they and why might you want to invest in one?

You might hear people talking about an exciting upcoming initial public offering, or IPO.

An IPO is the process a company goes through to become listed on a stock exchange so that members of the public can buy and sell its shares.

There are different reasons why a company might choose to offer an IPO. It might be excited about opportunities for future growth, and want to invest this money back into the company. On the other hand, an IPO provides a chance for existing shareholders (which might include employees, directors, and founders) to sell some — or all — of their shares in the company. If the company is raising money for this reason, it may suggest that the shareholders think it has reached a more mature phase, with opportunities for growth slowing down. Understanding the motivation for an IPO can help you to work out whether it's something you want to be part of.

Before a company lists on an exchange, like the New Zealand stock exchange (NZX), it's called a private company. Or, if it's owned by the government, a government entity. Once the company has been through the rigorous listing process, it's considered public.

IPOs can sometimes attract a lot of hype, particularly if it's a well-known company. This is something to watch out for — a high profile can result in a higher list price than you would otherwise expect, which can lead to disappointment if the price drops once the company starts trading.

Legal prep work

Before the company lists, an investment bank often helps it go through the legal steps required. The bankers are responsible for preparing the legal documents, finding investors to buy the initial shares, and lots of other things.

All of this prep work — and the rules and legal requirements — aim to protect shareholders and investors but they can be quite pricey for the company. Sometimes the cost of listing can deter a company from the IPO track.

An exchange sets the rules a private company needs to follow so it can list. Most exchanges have similar rules, but there can be differences around things like a company's minimum value and how trading happens. In New Zealand, the NZX provides rules and guidelines for companies that want to publicly list on its exchange. In Australia, the ASX fulfils that function.

Deciding on a share price

A company needs to do lots of research and analysis to figure out how much to sell its shares for.

If it sells shares for too little, it might not raise as much money as it could have. But if it sets the price too high, there might not be enough people who want to buy the shares.

Once a price is decided on, and the company has done all the necessary prep work, it can set a date for the IPO.

When shares start trading

Once a company lists, its shares can be bought or sold just like any other investment.

When trading starts, investors who took part in the IPO might benefit from a rise in the share price — or not.

An IPO can be oversubscribed. This means people want to buy more shares than a company is offering. If this happens, the offer might be scaled, which means investors may end up getting fewer shares than the amount they'd like to buy.

IPOs can be undersubscribed too, which means the company has offered more shares than people want to buy. If an IPO is undersubscribed, it's worth looking at why the demand is low.

When Facebook went public in May 2012, it listed at a price of US$38 per share. By September 2012, the share price had dropped below US$18 per share. Ouch. It took over a year to reach the IPO price again. By contrast, Allbirds (NASDAQ:BIRD) investors almost doubled their money from a list price of US$15 on the first day of trading in 2021 (but it has since dropped to below its listing price).

An IPO gives you the opportunity to invest in a company's shares while they're on the primary market. The primary market is where shares are issued for the first time. The shares go into the secondary market when they're listed and traded on a stock exchange.

What's market cap?

Market capitalisation, or market cap, is how much a company is worth, in total. You find it by multiplying the share price by the total number of shares that have been issued. This is useful because the number of shares plays a big role in determining how much a company is worth. After all, if you had a company with just one share, for $5000, it would be worth a lot less than a company with a million shares that cost $1 each.

Market capitalisation is really useful for comparing two companies against one another to figure out which one is more valuable.

Things to think about before taking part in an IPO

A company will release a document called a product disclosure statement (PDS) or prospectus before it lists. This gives potential investors key information about the company, like its financial position and performance. You can also find out why the company is making the offer, how it expects your investment to make a return, as well as any risks to the business that might affect your investment.

A PDS can be a chunky document to get through, so think about what you want to learn before you dive in.

Look at the company's financial track record and forecasts. Has it been consistently gaining customers, revenue and profit over the last few years, and do you think that the predicted growth is realistic?

Compare this to what the company thinks it is worth. In the PDS you should be able to find its implied market capitalisation value. This valuation should represent what the company's worth — but unfortunately, sometimes it doesn't. Are there similar companies that have wildly different valuations? You'll need to look outside of the PDS for this information.

Understand what the company will use the money it is raising for. It might want to pay off debt, use the money to fund growth opportunities, or allow existing shareholders to sell their shares. Do you think that the way the company is allocating money supports what it has planned for the future?

Think about what's happening in the industry. Is it a crowded market with lots of competitors? If so, what is this company doing differently?

Compare that to the company's strategy. Do you think it will be able to adapt and thrive over the next 10 years? How about 50?

Look at who's leading the company. What type of experience and skills do these people have?

Then, check what those leaders are doing with their shares. If the company is projected to grow, you'd think it's in their interests to hold on to their shares, right? The PDS will usually include an escrow arrangement. This outlines how long existing shareholders are required to hold their shares before they can sell them. If several shareholders plan to sell a large portion of their shares as part of the IPO, look into why they might be doing so.

While IPOs give you the opportunity to invest in a company before it lists, as with any investment, there are also associated risks. You should consider your risk appetite, and look at how these shares might fit within your wider investment strategy and portfolio.

Your wider investment strategy

There are lots of different strategies when it comes to investing. Some people like to go deep on companies' annual reports, some people like to read a share price chart, and some people like more set-and-forget approaches. And of course, there are all kinds of approaches and strategies in between.

Short-term versus long-term

You might have heard people talk about 'day traders' who spend their time very quickly buying and selling, trying to make a fast profit.

Research has found that 80 per cent of people buy investments or shares and hold on to them for the long term.[8] Just 2 per cent of people buy and sell multiple times a day.

Short-term trading is extra risky. Investing shouldn't be seen as a get-rich-quick scheme. Building wealth over time is a much more sustainable approach, with much less chance of being burned as you have more time to wait until a market recovers in the event of a downturn. (You may also have some tax implications to think about if you're investing purely with the intention of buying and selling for profit.)

There are lots of benefits to investing for the long term, and we hope you've picked up by now how much an investor can get out of simply having time on their side.

As we said earlier, time in the market, not timing the market, is usually what makes the biggest difference to your outcome. Time smooths out the glitches, wipes out the wobbles and allows any 'mistakes' to become a distant memory in an overall extremely successful investing strategy.

When you invest in shares for the short term, it becomes very important to buy and sell at precisely the right time — the pressure is on to buy just before prices go up, and sell just before prices go down. But this is really hard. People get it wrong all the time, which is expensive. Even people whose full-time job it is to pick investments find this difficult. If you're not sitting glued to a screen all day, watching market movements, how realistic is it that

---

8   'Retail investor platforms research', FMA (website), https://www.fma. govt.nz/news-and-resources/reports-and-papers/retail-investor- platforms-research/

you'll be able to spot the small market movements that short-term investors have to leap on?

By contrast, if you're going to sell in the distant future, it doesn't really matter if you buy your shares today, tomorrow or next week. If an investment is fundamentally good, it'll grow over the long term even if the value goes up and down in the short term.

If you're investing a little bit every week or so, the ups and downs matter even less, thanks to the dollar-cost averaging we discussed earlier. Over time, the amount you pay is smoothed out.

By investing for the long term, you can avoid the traps of daily market movements, because all you need is for the value of your investment to rise over a long period of time. The day-to-day and week-to-week movements aren't such a big deal, because you're in it for the long haul.

Longer-term investment also gives you more leeway to invest an amount you can afford.

When you're investing for the short term, you need to invest a larger amount to make it worth your while. If you invested $1, and made a 10 per cent return in a week, you'd have $1.10 at the end. That's a great percentage return, but it's not going to make a big difference in your life except if you're in the habit of trying to buy bottles of milk with cash.

But how are you meant to come up with $10,000 or $20,000 or an even bigger sum that would make that 10 per cent return really something worthwhile? You still have rent to pay, groceries to buy, fuel to put in your car.

Investing for the long term means you don't have to invest a large amount at once. Instead, you can invest a bit at a time, so your investments don't impact your day-to-day life too much. You might invest thousands of dollars in total, but at the rate of $50 or $100 or so a week. You can also increase that amount over time, and invest larger lump sums now and again, too.

By investing for a long period of time, you give yourself the time and financial space you need to build up to a large amount that will make a significant impact on your life. If you're not rich to start with, this is a lot easier than investing for the short term.

And remember that compound returns we talked about earlier? That really starts paying off when you invest for the long term.

Compound returns is one of the best things about investing for a long time. It's when you earn some interest or other returns, then start to earn returns from those returns. After a while, your returns are earning heaps of money just on their own, on top of the money you invested in the first place.

But it's impossible to get this benefit without investing for the long term, because your returns need time to grow.

Long-term investing suits those of us without a functioning crystal ball, too. As we've already explained, the market in general tends to increase in value over time. But you don't know the specifics of how it's going to go up and down along the way, and you don't know when these ups and downs are going to happen. Until your crystal ball is fully functioning, you're kind of just hoping for the best.

Of course, people who invest for the short term aren't highly qualified fortune-tellers, either. They make considered decisions, based on lots of research, conversations with experts, and years of their own experience to draw from. This can be time-consuming, expensive work. When you invest over a long time, you can just set and forget, and live your life — given that your investments are well diversified.

Here's another thing about that crystal ball: you don't know what your future financial life is going to look like. Hopefully, things will be looking good, and you'll have some security, your income will keep growing and you'll be in an even better financial position in five years' time, but you don't know that. What you do know is that you have some money to invest today. By investing for the long term, you're planning for your future. You may not know what that future looks like, but investing for the long haul is a great way to help make it a good one.

The upshot of this? You can invest short-term or long-term but we reckon the benefits of long-term investing are pretty clear.

Blue-chip approach

You may have heard the term 'blue chip', meaning something of the highest quality. A blue-chip company is an established public firm that is reasonably stable and has a strong record of steady growth — sometimes going back decades or more. On the NZX, the major banks are blue-chip companies, as are the major utilities companies. And on the ASX, the big four banks among some mining and telecommunications companies are labelled as blue-chip.

A blue-chip approach is exactly what it sounds like — it's investing a portion of your portfolio in these big-name companies that almost everyone has heard of and which historically have held pretty healthy balance sheets.

A blue-chip approach gives you a piece of companies that have historically been stable, have proven track records, and are highly liquid (meaning there's lots of shares being bought and sold every day). Although it's not guaranteed what they will do in the future, they have historically risen in value and delivered consistent dividends.

The downside of this approach is that you may miss out on some higher-risk growth opportunities. Many of these companies are long out of their rapid growth phase. But remember, there's nothing stopping you from following a blue-chip approach with some of your portfolio, and a different approach with different bits of your portfolio. It's about finding a strategy that works for you.

Another downside of this strategy is that 'blue chip' doesn't mean 'sure thing'. Blue-chip companies can lose value, and they can even (rarely) go bust, like Lehman Brothers (Lehman Brothers Holdings Inc.) in 2008.

Fundamental analysis

Fundamental analysis means investing in companies based on the fundamentals of how those companies are performing.

With fundamental analysis, it's important to remember that the best anyone can do is make an educated guess. You'll never be able to predict a company's future with 100 per cent certainty. Lots of fundamental investors hedge these educated guesses by staying diversified as well.

Fundamental analysis involves a lot of looking at annual reports, reading up on a company's competitors and getting familiar with some key metrics like income, revenue, cash flow and market capitalisation. You use these numbers to try and figure out if a share currently costs more or less than it's actually worth. If you think it costs less than it is worth, then it makes sense to buy it — after all, if it's worth a certain amount, you should eventually be able to sell it for that amount, once other people figure it out.

This is a great way to practise your business and finance skills, or build them up.

Investors use fundamental analysis when they think their analysis is telling a different, more accurate story than the one the rest of the market is hearing or believing. When investors buy shares based on fundamental analysis, they're essentially saying that they think a company is underpriced right now and will be worth more in the future. If you're doing fundamental analysis, you can make this decision based on just a few metrics, or significant research.

The main trade-off with fundamental analysis is that at best you are making a bit of an educated guess. To succeed at fundamental analysis, you have to be correct about how much a company's shares are worth when the rest of the market is wrong. After all, if you think some shares should be worth $5, but they're only trading for $3, you're telling everyone buying and selling those shares that they're doing so at the wrong price.

If you have the courage of your convictions, though, it may turn out really well — there are lots of situations where shares trade at prices that are lower than they should be, just because something has spooked other investors.

Technical analysis

Technical analysis is different from fundamental analysis. People following technical analysis are trying to time the market and focusing more on what other investors are doing than what the companies themselves are up to. They want to buy when prices are about to go up, and sell when prices are about to go down. This is really hard to predict, and people often get it wrong.

People who follow a technical analysis approach don't bother with things like annual reports or market research. Rather, they only look at two things: the share's price over time, and how many shares have been traded over time. Then, they try to find patterns in these two figures to signal an investment's strength or weakness.

You'll hear technical analysts talk about things like 'support' (when a share's price is heading down), 'resistance' (when a share's price is heading up) and 'head and shoulders'. 'Head and shoulders'

is the pattern on a line graph that looks like a head and shoulders
— the price rises, then falls back to where it was, then rises a bit
further, then falls back, then rises once more — but only to the
height of the first increase.

Head and Shoulders pattern

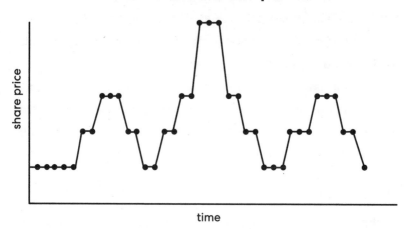

Investors who use technical analysis are saying that they think
past movements in a share's price are a good predictor of future
movements. If they're right, and they can pick the right moment to
jump in, they get rewarded with solid returns.

The main trade-off here is that you are trying to time the
market perfectly. What's more, you're trying to time the market
based only on what the share's price has done in the past. As we
all know, past share prices are not ever a guarantee about what the
shares will do in the future.

What now?

- Find an investing platform or way of investing that meets your needs. Sign up, have a look around and get familiar with how it works.
- Start digging around in the companies you might want to invest in — check out their recent financial statements and start to get acquainted with their plans.
- Practise reading through some annual reports to get used to the terminology that's being used.
- Think about what appeals to you — are there companies that stand out as being things you'd really like to be part of?
- Spend some time pondering what the world might look like in five or 10 years' time. What sort of companies do you think might do well in that environment? What can you start to get involved in now?
- Think about where your exposure is. Are all your financial interests in one country or industry? Do you need to spread your risk? Or have you made a definite decision to go 'all in' on something?
- Check out the funds available. Are there any that stand out as really aligning with your own investment interests or strategy?
- Consider what you want to do with your investment, in terms of building up your own financial position or helping the world around you. This will help you to work out what sort of investment strategy is right for you.
- Think about what feels right. What investment strategy makes you feel really excited about what comes next?

4.

What returns can you expect?

A big part of investing focuses on the reward you might eventually get. But what level of return is it reasonable to expect?

The answer, unfortunately, is: it depends. Some people invest for a short period of time and manage to make huge returns while other people invest for longer and see a more modest outcome, and returns aren't guaranteed.

There are lots of different things that can affect the returns you receive from your investment.

Returns from shares come in the two main ways we noted earlier.

- Capital gains — the value of your shares being worth more when you sell them than when you bought them.
- Dividends — money paid out to shareholders from the company's profits.

When you invest, you will probably be able to get an idea of whether a company is likely to give you a capital gain (often new companies or those in a growth phase) or dividends (usually established companies that have a solid run of profits).

Think of it as a pie. When you're investing for capital gains, you're investing in a pie and then that pie grows bigger, increasing the size of your slice along with it.

The dividends happen when the company makes a profit and shares that around — the pie itself isn't growing as much because bits of it are being cut off for shareholders to eat, but you still hold your slice.

The decision between whether you want some of the pie today or would rather hold on for a potentially bigger pie tomorrow will be driven by your circumstances and what you want from your investments.

Here are some things that can affect your return.

The level of risk you take

In the simplest terms, the return you get comes down to the risk you take. The more risk you're willing to manage, the more potential return you could receive.

You don't have to take the same amount of risk across all your investments. You might decide that for some of your money — maybe the amounts you're putting aside for a house deposit, say — you're not really willing to take much risk at all. But you might have another chunk of money available to you that you're more willing to take a moonshot with. ('Moonshot' is a word that's used to describe something that you get into without any real expectation of a profit in the near future but which could pay off a lot in the long run if everything goes to plan.) Your risk appetite changes a lot depending on the context.

People invest money for different reasons. In some ways, it's like shopping. Sometimes you buy the things you need, and sometimes you just buy the things you want.

We have set Sharesies up so that you don't have to have a minimum investment size, and you can put money into a whole lot of different things, for different reasons. This isn't always the case though — for example, a broker may require you to invest a minimum amount.

Your own behaviour

How you manage your investments can make a big difference to your returns, too. If you are the type of person who likes to trade frequently, your timing might not always line up with the gains that are possible. If you get worried and bail out when markets fall, you might miss out on the recovery.

But if you're an investor with a solid strategy and stick to it, you might be able to maximise your returns compared to others.

The length of time you're invested

Yep, we're back on that again.

The biggest factor that influences returns has been shown, time and again, to be the amount of time you spend in the market. Remember that compound returns we talked about earlier?

When you're an investor, compounding is your best friend. If you can put aside $20 a week for 50 years, with a 10 per cent return, you'll end up with more than $1.2 million.

But if you only have a 20-year time horizon, even $200 a week would get you to just over $620,000.

Compounding gives you returns on your returns — the closest thing to 'free money' you're probably going to see.

Staying invested for the long term also means you don't have to stress about making the right decision each month; with a diversified investment over a long period of time, things should always track up. Returns fluctuate and aren't guaranteed year to year, and in some cases your portfolio may dip, but the longer time you have to invest, there may be the opportunity to recover from those dips.

The wider world

As we've seen in recent years, what's going on in the rest of the financial world can really impact how your investments behave. When interest rates hit historic lows, many people put their money into shares because they could not get a return from the bank. That helped to support share prices, even when the world was dealing with significant uncertainty.

A pattern of growth over the long term

It's hard to say what is a 'normal' return to expect from a sharemarket investment.

You might say it's reasonable to expect you'd get a better return from shares than you would from leaving your money in the bank. But that depends on what sort of investor you are. If you pile all your money into one risky stock, there's actually a good chance you could end up worse off than you would be if you had the money in the bank.

(Although you could also do really well and significantly outperform.)

But if you have a well-diversified portfolio of sharemarket investments across different sectors and industries, you'll be better able to weather whatever happens on the market.

People sometimes talk about 8 per cent per year being an 'average' return. But if you invest in a high-growth stock that goes well, you could shatter that 8 per cent and end up with a return of hundreds of per cent. But you could end up with zero.

The rubber band between those two things is the risk involved. The further the rubber band is stretched and the less certain something is, the more you could gain.

If you could never lose money, your returns would match the bank. If you want to get outside that, you need to increase your risk.

But if you think back to that innate optimism that comes with investing, which we discussed earlier, you'll understand why the long-term theme is growth.

When you're investing, you're backing a better future. If you believe and can identify the ingenuity of humans to adapt and grow, and find ways to innovate to create a better world, there will be growth. You might have ups and downs but the longer the time horizon, the greater the opportunity.

People's need for things and services won't change. The needs and services themselves might, but the reality is that people will need stuff, and will need things done, and companies will evolve and grow to cater to those needs.

Over the past 120 years, New Zealand and Australian sharemarkets have been among the best performers in the world. Between 1900 and 2020, New Zealand's sharemarket had a return of 6.5 per cent a year and Australia 6.8 per cent.

New Zealand has traditionally had a stock exchange dominated by dividend stocks rather than high-growth ones. That's starting to change with the emergence of companies like Xero (ASX: XRO), which really helped to change the New Zealand psyche about growth companies.

Penny stocks

You might have heard of people taking a gamble on penny stocks and making a mint. (Remember Leonardo DiCaprio's character spruiking them in *The Wolf of Wall Street*?)

We're a lot more into investing in businesses we care about and building that investment up over time rather than trying to bet on a minnow making it big. But if you're keen to dabble in this part of the market, there are some things you should know.

A 'penny stock' is a company with very inexpensive shares. You'll also sometimes hear them referred to as 'small cap' companies, but generally a penny stock is taking this to the extreme. That means their total worth (share price multiplied by the number of shares issued) is much less than some of the bigger companies.

The companies are usually quite niche and their shares are often bought and sold infrequently, which means the share price can be really volatile and the shares might be illiquid. This means if you want to sell penny stock shares, you may have to wait for a buyer — or instead, sell at a discount. Or if you want to buy, you may have to pay a premium for your order to be filled. The other people who own the penny stock shares are in the same situation. This means that the price can go up and down really quickly as people either buy up shares at a premium, or offload them at a discount — even if nothing has changed with the underlying company.

Penny stocks might be new companies without a track record.

One benefit of investing in penny stocks is found in their name — they don't cost much to buy into. In some cases, they could grow and become worth significantly more in the future. But that also comes with risk. Their share price can move around a lot and potentially the shares could become completely worthless.

Small mining companies can be an example of a speculative penny stock. The company might own some land (or the rights to dig up some land) that may have valuable minerals in it, without knowing if the minerals are actually there or not.

If it finds minerals, the company could be worth a lot more than it currently is, because it will be able to sell those minerals for a lot of money. But if it doesn't, then the company could effectively be worth nothing.

Another example could be a medicine company looking to get approval from the authorities to sell a new drug. If it gets approval, then it could be worth more than it is now, as it brings a new drug to market. If it doesn't, then the company won't be able to sell anything — and again, its shares could be worth nothing.

It's the same situation as companies looking to file a patent for a new product. If they get the patent, they'll have exclusive rights to sell whatever it is they've invented. But if the patent isn't granted, then the company's idea can be copied by anyone — making its road to success a lot harder.

While investing in penny stock companies may come with growth potential, it can also come with significant risk.

If you're going to invest in penny stocks, think about why they might be so cheap. After all, even a cheap share is too expensive if it's worth nothing in six months. Penny stocks may come with opportunity, but as with all investing that opportunity comes with risk.

Blue-chip companies

The opposite of a penny stock is a blue-chip company.

As mentioned earlier, a blue-chip company is a publicly listed company that is well established and has a strong record of steady growth.

They're the big-name companies that you'll have heard of — companies like the banks, Coca-Cola (The Coca-Cola Company NYSE:KO) and IBM (International Business Machines Corporation NYSE:IBM). Their share price tends to be comparatively stable. Blue-chips may grow in value over time, but they tend to do so at a steady pace, rather than big movements up and down.

They tend to be older companies. You don't become a blue-chip company overnight. Blue-chip companies have had many years to develop their business and build a strong reputation.

While penny stocks have a small market cap, blue chips are the companies with larger market capitalisations (total value of all the shares), usually paying regular dividends.

One of the main reasons investors like blue-chip companies is because they may be lower risk compared to newer, untested companies. You can have some certainty over their performance (although nothing is ever completely guaranteed) and know that it's likely, though not guaranteed, they'll produce a pretty steady stream of dividends to shareholders.

Basically, a blue-chip company is like a person with a big savings account; if they lose their job, they can fall back on the savings account while they find another one. A newer entrant is more similar to a person with no savings account, or even lots of credit-card debt — if they lose their job, things can go from bad to worse really quickly.

So investing in blue-chip companies is a good way to get a higher chance of stable investments, because generally, blue-chip companies are less risky than other investments.

The main trade-off is to do with growth. Blue-chip companies may grow slowly, or not at all, because most are at or near the point where they are as big as they are going to get. They are unlikely to grow significant amounts quickly, and they are unlikely to have their value swing up and down in the short term. You're not likely to quickly double your money with an investment in a blue-chip stock.

Cycles

Research has shown there are some patterns that sharemarkets historically follow, but as with any investment, past returns are no guarantee of future performance and a lot of the things that used to be seen as a pretty clear rule have started to look less guaranteed.

There are usually four phases of a market cycle: prices increase, peak, flatten out, dip and then begin to rise again. This can happen over a period of days, months or years.

Accumulation (prices increase)

This is the period after a market fall when things settle down a bit and people start to come back into the market, slowly starting to push prices up from their lows. This is the time that people usually look back on and think: 'I wish I'd invested a bit more money back then, before things really took off and got expensive.'

The biggest challenge for investors through this period is often having the confidence to put money in while others are holding back. You'll still often hear a lot of negative market commentary in the media at this point in a cycle, so knowing what you are doing and why is really important. Over this period, market sentiment will start to change back to something a bit more neutral.

Mark-up (prices peak)

During this phase, the market starts to move higher and more potential buyers jump in, and the rest of the world cottons on to the fact that things are looking up for the markets. As it progresses, more and more people have the confidence to buy — there is usually a 'selling climax' in the last stages of this period as the last group of people who've been hanging back feel the FOMO and jump in — prompting big share price increases in a relatively short period of time.

This is the time when people are being driven by some of the less admirable emotions, like greed and fear, and some experienced investors might start to think that the prices are getting too high, and cash in.

Distribution (prices flatten)

In this phase, sellers become the dominant players in the market, trying to take their gains and get out. Sometimes prices pick up again and then level off many times during this period.

Mark-down (prices dip)

This is when prices start to fall more clearly — some people hold on in the hope that things will recover, but eventually the prices drop to the point where many investors bail. When enough are selling out, confident traders start to buy again, which moderates prices before they begin to move into the accumulation phase again.

The bull market (explained shortly) seen around the world in the decade after the Global Financial Crisis was the longest in history — although Covid-19 caused a bit of volatility that investors had to hold on through.

ASX 200 movement 2012-2022

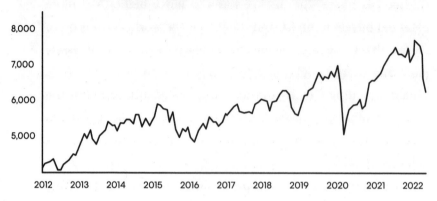

Success stories

There's something a bit bittersweet about looking back at investment returns and working out where you should have put your
money a decade ago. But it can be inspiring, too, to try to spot the
next big things that might be hovering around out there now.

Between 2009 and 2019, A2 Milk Company Limited (ASX:AZM,
NZTX:ATM) was one of the big success stories of the New Zealand
market. A $100 investment in 2009 would have turned into almost
$20,000 by 2019. Mainfreight Limited (NZX: MFT) was another share
that had strong growth over the period, rising from $5.55 to $41.70.

Their performance has varied since 2019, though. A2's share
price fell from a high of more than $20 in mid-2020 to about $6 by mid-
2022. Mainfreight has continued a steady climb, apart from a period
of disruption as Covid-19 hit New Zealand. Its share price topped
$90 by mid-2021 (and had fallen back to under $70 by mid-2022).

On the US sharemarket, Amazon.com Inc. (NASDAQ:AMZN)
also did well — it recorded growth of more than 333 per cent over
the five years to mid-2021.

There have been some standout funds, too. The Kiwi Wealth Growth KiwiSaver fund has returned 11.1 per cent a year over 10 years to June 2021. SuperLife's High Growth fund returned 31 per cent over one year to June 2021. Milford's Active Growth fund returned 14.1 per cent a year over 10 years.

If someone invested $10,000 in the Vanguard ESG US Stock ETF (ESGV) in 2017, it would have been worth almost $17,000 in August 2021. But while these companies have performed well in the past, there isn't a guarantee they'll keep growing this way. So do your research, and make sure the company meets your investing strategy.

Bulls and bears

When you're interested in investing, you'll probably hear people talking about 'bull markets' or things turning 'bearish'. Don't worry, no wild animals are involved.

A bull market is a market in which prices are rising, or are expected to. People are confident and optimistic.

A bear market is the reverse — it's a market where there are prolonged price declines. Usually, markets have to drop 20 per cent or more, with negative investor sentiment, to be classed as a bear market.

Bulls and bears are both based on prices. Prices are driven by how much people want shares. If they really want shares, they'll be willing to pay more for them; if they don't really want shares, they won't be willing to pay that much.

More than that, it's probably saying something about the overall economy. When things are generally going well, companies will be more profitable. It follows that more people would want to invest in these companies — after all, they're doing well.

This means that the opposite is true, too. If the economy is not doing well, then companies aren't doing that well either — and people aren't going to want to invest in companies that aren't doing very well. If they do invest in them, they won't be prepared to pay that much to do so.

You can also get bulls and bears solely from how people think the sharemarket is tracking. If people think the market is crashing, they might panic and start selling at whatever price they can get. As more people sell, prices start to drop — even if the companies underneath are doing well. And the reverse can happen, too. If people get a surge of confidence, they might start buying up shares, even if the companies represented by those shares aren't actually in great shape.

These tend to be shorter-term bulls and bears, as the reality of the underlying situation will eventually become clear.

Your own behaviour might drive returns

A big part of your eventual investment outcome is your own behaviour.

Research shows that the way people act with their investments can play a huge role in their overall investment success. You might have heard people talk about 'behavioural economics'. This has come to the fore in recent years. Traditionally, most financial theory relies on the assumption that everyone involved in the market is a 'rational actor' who never makes a mistake, and makes all their decisions based on perfect calculations and full access to all the possible information available to them.

But clearly, that's not actually the case. People often do things that seem inexplicable in hindsight, or at least a little strange.

Behavioural finance steps in and tries to explain how human emotions influence investment decisions.

In 2015, research firm DALBAR released some data that showed average investors consistently failed to achieve returns in line with market indices. It found the average equity mutual fund investor underperformed the S&P 500 by a wide margin of 8.19 per cent.[9]

A big reason that is often cited is that people buy high and sell low, even if they say they are trying to do the opposite. They'll jump into the market when sentiment is good and prices are high, then get spooked when things wobble and prices drop. (When you hear someone say 'This time it's different', that's a good indication that their behaviour might cost them some returns down the track!)

Here are a few behaviours to watch out for if you want to maximise your returns and minimise the potential for unhelpful behaviours to get in the way:

The rule of 72

You might have heard of the rule of 72.[10] It's a quick formula that helps you work out how many years it will take to double your money at any rate of return.

Divide 72 by the rate of return you're getting (this works best for returns between about 6 per cent and 10 per cent) and the answer is the number of years.

A return of 4 per cent (72 divided by 4) means your investment may take 18 years to double.

---

9 'DALBAR'S 22nd Annual Quantitative Analysis of Investor Behaviour', https://fpai.net/wp-content/uploads/2018/01/2016-Dalbar-QAIB-Report.pdf

10 Luca Pacioli — 1494 book *Summa de arithmetica, geometria, proportioni et proportionalita (Summary of Arithmetic, Geometry, Proportions, and Proportionality)*.

Confirmation bias

This is when you only seek out views that you agree with, without seriously looking at any opposing information. Economist Zoe Wallis gives this example: 'If I think Apple [Apple Inc. NASDAQ:AAPL] is the best company out there then I'm more likely to read articles talking about what an amazing chief executive Tim Cook is, and how the latest iPhone release is going to be phenomenal.

'I'm less likely to look at negative reviews about battery life and the latest operating system update . . . or look seriously at their major competitors who have made huge gains in the smartphone space.'

You often see this sort of thing happening in friend groups where everyone has a similar outlook and experience. You form similar views, discuss those together and convince yourself that your opinion is the correct one, and cannot imagine anyone else having a different view. Social media is often criticised for reinforcing world views in this way. You get into your bubble, decide you're right and can't comprehend any other point of view.

This is as dangerous in the investing world as it can be in the political world. You can counter this by going out and looking for the viewpoints of people who disagree with you, or get someone to play devil's advocate while you discuss your thoughts.

Familiarity bias

This is similar to confirmation bias. We're most likely to invest in things that we're familiar and comfortable with. (Just have a look at the property market!)

But while it's great to invest in things that you know well and understand, this can create issues with diversification. If you're piling all your money into stocks listed in your own country, or in a particular type of industry, you're more exposed to a downturn if something affects that country or sector.

Try not to put all your eggs in one basket (remember the Super Chicken story?) and think about how you can spread your risk.

FOMO

We've heard a lot about FOMO lately — it stands for Fear Of Missing Out. When share prices are getting hot, people start to talk about them a lot more.

There's a saying that when a random person in a lift is talking about share prices, that means it's time to get out. This represents the idea that when there's a lot of buzz and hype about something, it's worth being a bit cautious. Are you buying because the fundamentals are good, or because everyone else is sure they're on to a good thing, and you don't want to miss out?

Another 'fear of' that might reduce your returns is the fear of regret.

If you bought a share at a certain price, you don't want to regret that decision when you're forced to sell for a lower price, so you hang on. If you bought a share for $20 and it drops to $10, you might hang on and not sell until it gets back to $20. But if something fundamental has changed for the company, its share price might not get back to $20 again and you are better to sell at $10 than ride a decline further.

You might also have looked at a company, decided not to buy, and then its share price went on to rise significantly. You don't want to regret missing out on buying it earlier, so you don't buy in later — missing out on further price gains. Avoiding regret might lead to more regret later on!

You can challenge these fears by carefully looking at the share prices and fundamentals of each company you are invested in. If you already hold the stock, are you happy that you would buy it again at that price, if you didn't already own it? If you are considering buying it, does the performance of the company — or its outlook — justify the price? Even if you missed out on the lowest price, is there still room for further growth?

Loss aversion

No one likes to lose money, right?

Research has shown that we feel the pain of losing money much more keenly than we feel the benefit of an investing win. A loss can be twice as painful as the positive feeling of a gain.

Bizarrely, that can actually lead to us ending up with less money over the long run.

This feeling drives people to spend their money now, rather than invest or save it. We can feel the loss of missing out on shopping now, even though we could end up with more in the long term. If we suffer an investment loss, we're likely to hang on and wait for a gain. If we get a gain, we're likely to take a small profit than hold on for a longer-term, bigger gain.

You can counter this by setting yourself a clear timeframe for your investment. If you're investing in riskier assets like shares, tell yourself you're in it for five years or more and be prepared to ride out any volatility — review regularly and when your personal circumstances change.

Overconfidence

Positivity and optimism are good — but overconfidence can lead to some less than ideal investing decisions.

Humans sometimes overestimate the chance of good things happening and downplay the possibility of bad things happening. Try to consider the risks of your investments as well as the opportunities, and understand what return you can reasonably expect.

Over- and under-reacting

On a related note, investors often get too optimistic when markets are going up and assume that rise will continue indefinitely. Extreme overreacting, like investing a lot of money in a company that's seen stock-price growth without any real story to back it up, can lead to price crashes.

Investors can also become extremely pessimistic when things turn downwards and assume that trend will continue, when in reality it's just a short-term blip. (You might hear people talk about 'anchoring' — putting too much weight on things that have happened recently without considering historical data.)

But while those investing behaviours can get in the way of success, there are also some that set you up for a win. And the success of long-term investing has a lot to do with behaviours.

Good habits

If you can get into positive investor habits, they will help you to shine. With a good rhythm of investing even a small amount week after week, or month after month, you're more likely to do well over the long term.

Worry less about daily news

Research has shown that individuals are better investors when they hold for the long term and aren't trying to be day traders or aggressively outperform. Women in particular tend to be good at this — they don't trade often but they do want their money to work really hard for them. There's a definite advantage in knowing your strategy, knowing why you've chosen a particular company to invest in and quietly staying the course while other people run around madly chasing the next big thing.

People can end up buying high and selling low if they let too much of the market noise take up space in their brains.

We're not saying you should stick your head in the sand. You'll need to respond to news, rather than react. When you hear something new about your investments, consider whether it changes anything about your strategy. Does the information change the reason why you invested in that company? If it does, that's a fair reason to sell. But if it doesn't, just hold on and stick to your strategy.

Cyclical stocks and non-cyclical stocks

You can help to lessen the impact of market movements on your portfolio by investing in a spread of 'cyclical' and 'non-cyclical' stocks.

Cyclical stocks are companies that feel the pain when there's an economic downturn. They include luxury retailers who might suffer if unemployment is up and people are worried about splashing out on a pricey handbag, or travel providers who might see people cutting back on their holidays.

Non-cyclical stocks are companies that keep on trucking and turning good profits, no matter what the wider market is doing. These types of companies include power companies and supermarkets — people have to be able to turn on their lights and feed their families regardless of the economic situation.

Don't invest what you can't afford to lose?

Some people will tell you that you shouldn't invest money you can't afford to lose.

That might be true if your 'investing' is buying Lotto tickets.

But it doesn't have to be the case for investing in assets like shares and funds.

The most important part of that phrase is the word 'afford'. This has nothing to do with the amount of money you invest, but is actually about 'impact'. What would be the impact on you if your investment were to lose value?

Every investment you make has a risk of not giving you the returns you expect or to decrease in value. The higher your expected returns, the more risk you generally take to achieve those returns. Taking more risk gives you a chance at higher returns, while taking less risk reduces your likelihood of getting higher returns.

The impact of a risk is much more important — in other words, what you might be willing to lose for the potential of an upside, and how long you can manage holding that loss? To figure out the answer to this question, you need to ask yourself what would happen if your investment decreased in value, today.

If all the money in your transaction account at the bank decreased in value, that would have a very significant impact on you — you might struggle to pay your rent or cover your grocery bill at the supermarket. But if you had some money invested in a fund with the intention of keeping it there for 10 years anyway, the impact of a day-to-day fluctuation would be insignificant. You might not even notice.

Of course, there's still the risk of the investment not giving you the returns you want over the 10-year period. But by investing for that longer time horizon, the ups and downs along the way won't have as much impact.

By finding ways to reduce the impact of a risk, you may be able to accept a higher chance of a loss in the shorter term, for a chance of a higher return in the longer term.

Diversification is another way to increase the amount you can afford. Let's say you have $100 to invest. If you put that entire $100 into one investment that has a high likelihood of losing some of its value, then the impact of that high risk is pretty high — in the worst case, you could lose your entire $100.

If you split the $100 into two parcels, and put one in a risky investment and one in a less risky investment, then you would be cutting the potential impact in half. You're more likely to lose $50 than to lose the entire $100.

You can then split this as many times as you want — you can even invest in a fund to split it into 500 chunks, or more!

The point is that diversification helps to reduce the potential impact of any one investment choice losing value. The likelihood of it losing value doesn't change, but the impact on you of the loss in value does.

So when you look at it this way, the phrase 'Don't invest what you can't afford to lose' is technically true. But only technically. Investing money that you don't care about losing is one way to reduce the impact of the risks you're taking, but it's not the only way.

You can achieve the same goal, invest more, and get access to potentially higher returns, by investing with a longer time horizon and making sure you've managed your risk through diversification.

Investor story: In it for the long haul

Melanie started investing in Sharesies in 2018. She says that it seemed like an easy way to get started. 'It seemed like an easy platform for me to use. I don't have heaps of money so I didn't want to use a person . . . I didn't have enough to warrant hiring a broker. But I was always interested in business and profit and the excitement of seeing a business grow.'

Being able to start with as little as $5 was a big part of the appeal. 'Sharesies made it very easy and user-friendly. Then from there you start branching out, looking at other things and taking more control yourself.'

Melanie says the Sharesies offer grew alongside her interest. When she started, it was only possible to invest in funds via the platform. 'You couldn't invest in individual businesses, then as your interest might be waning, all of a sudden they release all the shares on the New Zealand stock exchange, then the American stock exchange and then the Australian stock exchange. They kept releasing more companies [to invest in] — that kept the interest there.'

Melanie says she doesn't have an overriding investment strategy but always tries to hold things for the long term.

'I went through a phase thinking I want to have at least one share in every company that I was interested in. That included things like Amazon.com Inc. [NASDAQ:AMZN] and Apple Inc. [NASDAQ:AAPL], some of the bigger American companies that cost hundreds of dollars for one share. That was one little goal then, trying to buy those at the right time so I wasn't buying at a high each time. Keeping an eye on them, waiting until it was low, adding a bit more then a bit more until I got one share. That [strategy has] gone by the by because some of those shares are hugely expensive. But I've noticed I'm making lots of money from those ones as it is without having an actual full share in it.

'Other times I might look at what the company does, looking for sustainable companies. I went through another phase of researching individual companies and learnt about companies I'd never heard of, then I'd invest in them and watch them. When the Australian shares came up I thought Australia's known for its mining so I went into a few mining companies there. It's been hit and miss with those.'

Melanie says her nursing background meant she was interested in healthcare stocks and she invested in Pfizer Inc. (NYSE:PFE) quite early in her investing career.

She also keeps up with media coverage of business issues and when a name keeps coming up, she will look into it to see whether it is a worthwhile investment. Sometimes she finds companies by word of mouth.

'My strategy changes all the time. But I tend not to sell. I tend to just keep buying. That's probably the overriding strategy.'

She says while some investors had done better than her over the time, they might be spending a lot more time and taking it more seriously. 'I have always just had fun with it and I've never been upset with any minuses because I'm only putting in what I can afford to lose. I'm not putting in huge chunks at a time.'

Melanie thinks market volatility often presents a good time to buy. 'I think it's really important to keep it so that you're having fun. My parents were big investors and they lost a lot in the 1980s crash. I always remember how devastated they were. I thought, "I never ever want to be in that situation."

'I was quite nervous when I first went into it but I feel as though I'm the one in control of it even though I have no control whatsoever, apart from controlling how much money I put in.'

What now?

- Check you understand what you're investing in and what level of risk and return you might expect from your investments.
- It's OK to take different levels of risk with different parts of your investment portfolio. You probably wouldn't put your life savings in one risky stock but if you have a smaller amount you're happy to have a go with, you might like the opportunity for a gain that a riskier investment creates.
- Have a strategy in mind, even if it's a simple 'buy and hold'.
- When you hear information about your investments, weigh it up — does it change the fundamentals of why you invested? If so, consider selling. If not, stay the course.
- Don't try to time the market. It's really hard to get it right.
- Don't worry too much about what other people are doing. What matters is making investment decisions that work for you.

5.

Should you buy local or international shares?

As you progress through your investing journey, you might start wondering whether you should invest in local firms or start looking further afield, investing in some big-name international companies.

At Sharesies, we started off by offering a handful of ETFs, before expanding to add NZX-listed companies, then added US and Australian investments. This means, even if you're based in Sydney or Te Whanganui-a-Tara Wellington, you can now invest in Tesla, Inc. (NASDAQ:TSLA) or Amazon.com Inc. (NASDAQ:AMZN) just as easily as you could in Australian and New Zealand Banking Group Limited (ASX:ANZ).

You can also put your cash into funds that invest in Europe, Japan and emerging markets like China, India and Brazil.

The main reason that people look offshore for investments is diversification and a wider range of opportunities. Diversifying your investments across countries and industries gives you a broader exposure, and lessens your overall risk.

If you invest in multiple companies based all in the same country, you're slightly diversified in that you're not overly exposed to the ups and downs of a single company. You might see your tech stocks doing well while your tourism ones struggle, for example. Or your healthcare stocks might do well while your retail ones are a bit softer.

But you're not diversified from things happening in that country that affect many companies — such as changes to laws and regulations, what's happening in the economy or even natural disasters.

If you were invested entirely in New Zealand companies and, hypothetically, the New Zealand government introduced a new tax on company profits, this could negatively impact the profits of the New Zealand-based companies in your portfolio and the value of the shares that you hold.

But if your investments were spread across other countries (including investments in companies in countries that weren't affected by the tax changes), the impact on your overall portfolio would be reduced. The value of the New Zealand portion might fall but the other areas would probably hold their value.

If you live in Australia and were fully invested in Australian companies and something happened to the Australian economy, your job could be affected, and the value of your house if you own one there. But if your investments are in another country, they might be unscathed.

New Zealand and Australian investors tend to like to invest in each other's countries, and some investments in the United States. That is probably because these countries feel quite familiar and safe. We usually spend a bit of time in each other's countries and know the brands that are household names. US companies seep into our consciousness through a lot of the media we consume, and because so many of them reach their tentacles into our economies, too.

While the Aotearoa and Australian economies are somewhat intertwined, they're still two separate economies — so investing in both gives you a greater opportunity to be diversified than investing in just one of them.

For New Zealanders, international diversification can be even more important than for investors in other countries. While there is a range of companies on the NZX, it is still a small country that is relatively exposed to international risk.

With Australia being a larger country, there are more investment opportunities — with more than 2000 companies listed on the ASX, compared to fewer than 200 on the NZX.

This means that the New Zealand stock exchange doesn't cover as many industries as the Australian stock exchange — if you want to invest in something like the financial sector, you'll get a much wider range of opportunities in Australia.

There are also more large companies on the Australian stock exchange (ASX). In July 2021, there were only two companies on the NZX with a market capitalisation higher than NZ$50 billion. On the ASX at the same time, there were nine companies with a market capitalisation of more than A$50 billion and three with market capitalisations higher than A$100 billion.

Australia offers a good initial diversification opportunity for New Zealand investors. In return, Australian investors might want to add Kiwi growth stocks, or some of the tried-and-true infrastructure companies, for a bit of variation in their portfolios.

But investors in both countries tend to look to the United States when they want to add a bit more international flavour.

Think of the big-name companies that you deal with all the time in your life — Apple Inc. (NASDAQ:AAPL), maybe, or Amazon. com Inc. (NASDAQ:AMZN), Facebook Inc. (now Meta Platforms Inc. NASDAQ:META) or Google (Alphabet Inc.) (NASDAQ:GOOGL). These are all companies that are listed in the United States.

Many investors in our part of the world also like to invest in the United States because of the resources that are available there.

When companies think about growing in Australia or New Zealand, they are still a little limited in the amount of growth they can achieve before they have to start looking offshore for capital and growth opportunities. That's not the case for US companies, which have a huge market both in consumers and investors to play in as they develop.

You might also find that there are more opportunities to pursue niche investment interests in bigger international markets.

Of course, the world isn't made up solely of New Zealand, Australia and the United States.

There are investment opportunities all over the globe. Understanding what's available to you as an investor in each market can help you to work out how those companies fit into your investing strategy.

Broadly, we talk about international opportunities being in three main camps: big developed economies; smaller developed economies; and emerging economies.

Let's explore these different types of economies a bit more.

Big developed economies

A developed economy is an economy where most of the basics are taken care of. Laws and contracts are enforced, so people can open businesses with more certainty. Important infrastructure like electricity is in place, and it's reliable — when you flick the light switch, the lights go on, every time. People are generally well educated, so if you want to hire someone, you can rely on them having basic skills like reading and writing.

On top of this, some of the developed economies are really large. Think of places like the USA, Japan and Germany. They're highly populated, and they produce really valuable goods and services that they sell to the whole world. The US is the world's biggest equity market by a significant margin — it is 56 per cent of the world's free-float market capitalisation[11] (that's the total value of all shares on issue around the world). Japan, at 7.4 per cent, is a distant second.

Toyota Motor Corporation (NYSE:TM) is based in Japan. Toyota factories are worldwide, but whenever a car rolls off the line and gets sold, the profits flow back to Japan. Same goes for iPhones (US) and even Best Foods Mayonnaise (manufactured by Unilever plc NYSE:UL), a British/Dutch company).

The benefit of investing in these really big developed economies is that you get a piece of the richest companies in the world, with access to consumers who often have comparatively large amounts of disposable income to spend. What's more, the big players in these economies sell things all over the world. This helps insulate them from local economic issues because there's money coming in from all over the place.

If there's a downturn in demand for Toyota cars in Japan, the

---

11 'Press Release: Credit Suisse Global Investment Returns Yearbook 2021', Credit Suisse (website), https://www.credit-suisse.com/about-us-news/en/articles/media-releases/credit-suisse-global-investment-returns-yearbook-2021-202103.html

company will probably be supported by ongoing orders from the United States or Europe.

It's relatively easy for investors in our part of the world to invest in these economies. As you already know, you can buy shares in lots of US companies through Sharesies, or other investing platforms. For example, an ETF like Vanguard's Large Cap Index Fund (NYSEARCA:VV) will instantly put you into a basket of big-name US companies. Smartshares' Japan Equities ESG ETF (NZX:JPN) will put you in 300 companies in the Japanese market.

The potential downside in focusing on these big economies when it comes to investing is there can be less room for growth — you're more likely to hear shares being described as 'over-valued' in the bigger markets. People sometimes also complain that developed markets are 'overcrowded'.

Smaller developed economies

While there are only a few big developed economies in the world, there is also plenty of smaller developed economies. These are economies that have the same features as the larger ones (good infrastructure, reliable laws, educated people), but they don't have the enormous numbers of people that the big economies do, and they're not as rich.

New Zealand is a good example. Finland, Denmark and Ireland are others that people often mention.

Some smaller developed economies are export-driven. This means they make a good chunk of their total money by selling products to other economies.

Australia exports lots of natural resources like gold, iron and coal. These things are valuable, but they also cost a lot to get in the first place, and the end product is less valuable. Imagine how much more a truck full of iPhones would sell for compared to a truck full of iron.

The iShares MSCI Denmark ETF Fund (EDEN) will give you instant exposure to the Denmark sharemarket. It's been a solid performer, returning almost 130 per cent in the five years to the end of 2021 (keeping in mind that past performance isn't an indication for future performance).

Emerging economies

There are also a lot of opportunities in the economies that are still developing. They're building infrastructure and educating their citizens, and they're starting to sell really valuable stuff to the world. Examples of these include China, India and Brazil. China is the biggest emerging market in the world. China's weight in the benchmark MSCI Emerging Markets Index doubled over the five years to 2021.[12]

The big advantage of investing in these economies is that they can be more affordable than investing in developed economies and the opportunities for growth can be phenomenal.

In a developing market, you can get involved much earlier in the growth story and ride the wave of development and increasing wealth. If China, for example, is able to become as developed as the USA, that is potentially more than a billion people, all contributing to a hugely valuable whole.

---

12 'Is it time to drop China from emerging market indices? Easier said than done', South China Morning Post (website), https://www.scmp.com/comment/opinion/article/3156471/it-time-drop-china-emerging-market-indices-easier-said-done

If you'd invested $100 in 1950 when the USA S&P 500 was starting to really emerge, it would have been worth about $15,000 by 2019. That's the benefit of getting in early for an emerging economy — but that benefit comes with risk, too.

Building infrastructure and educating citizens is hard, expensive and takes ages. And it's not a sure thing, either. Some economies never quite manage to emerge, or take a really long time to do so, which means the companies in those economies don't have the same ability to create value that companies in developed economies have.

But the upside is that investing in an emerging economy is potentially getting in on the ground floor of huge growth.

Investors can get exposure to emerging markets via Sharesies through investing in funds. There are lots of options available. For example, Vanguard FTSE Emerging Markets Stock Index FundETF returned 39.17 per cent over five years to September 2021. The Smartshares Emerging Markets ETF (NZX:EMF) returned 43.96% per cent over the same period (both excluding dividends paid by the fund).

Emerging vs developed markets

While past performance is no indicator of future returns, we can look at what's happened in the past to get a sense of what sort of factors affect the returns of different economies.

Credit Suisse's Global Investment Returns Yearbook says emerging markets outperformed in the early part of the twentieth century but were knocked about by the 1917 Russian Revolution and collapsed in the period of 1945–49 — Japanese equities lost 97 per cent of their value in US dollar terms in that post-war period.[13] But in the period between 1960–2020, emerging markets' annualised return was 11.2 per cent compared to 9.5 per cent for developed markets, based on Credit Suisse's representative indexes.

At the turn of the century, emerging markets were less than 3 per cent of the world equity market capitalisation and 24 per cent of GDP. Today they are 14 per cent of the free-float investable universe of world equities, Credit Suisse says, and 43 per cent of GDP.

Some commentators say that the emerging markets could exhibit more strength over the next 10 years, because those markets have a lot of room to increase their GDP per capita. Healthcare businesses in developing economies are tipped to shine, in particular.

What do you need to know before you invest offshore?

Wherever you're investing, you'll need to do the same sort of due diligence that you would expect on any investment.

Have a clear understanding of what you are investing in, and why.

It's tempting to see the big names of the American companies you know so well and think that they'll be a sure bet. But it helps to build up your knowledge of the fundamentals of the investment, whether it's a household name or something you haven't really come across much before, so that if new information comes to light you know how to handle it.

If you're really passionate about investing in things that align

---

13   'Credit Suisse Global Investment Returns Yearbook 2019', https://www.credit-suisse.com/media/assets/corporate/docs/about-us/research/publications/csri-summary-edition-credit-suisse-global-investment-returns-yearbook-2019.pdf

with your values, you might want to search news stories about the investments on your shortlist. Then you can ask yourself if those companies and ETFs are doing things that line up with your core beliefs.

Or if you're particularly interested in digging into the details of a company, you could read their annual report or financial results — you can find these on the relevant company or stock exchange's website.

The big difference is in scale. Since there are a lot more companies and ETFs in the US, there's a lot more information to find. This is a good thing, because there's more sources of specialised business information and analysis for you to take a look at.

One great place to start is to set up a Google (Alphabet Inc.) (NASDAQ:GOOGL) Alert for any companies or sectors you're interested in. You'll get an email every time they get mentioned in the news, which helps to paint a picture over time.

There are also a bunch of places you can go to find financial news and analysis, such as business and financial news sites, or email newsletters about the sharemarket.

Once you're invested, make a habit of checking these every now and again, because not all the news about international companies and investment markets makes it to Australia or New Zealand.

Foreign exchange

Now we get to the thing that can add a bit of complexity to your investment in overseas shares (and, to a lesser extent, funds): foreign exchange.

It's just like when you're shopping while you're on holiday. Buying a top for US$20 when you're in Hawaii might seem cheap, until you realise that the New Zealand dollar has fallen since you got on the plane and that same top is effectively costing you NZ$32 when you'd previously expected NZ$25.

Usually, when you invest in shares overseas (or a fund does on your behalf) you will use the local currency of the exchange that you are buying through.

When you buy US shares on an American stock exchange, you change your local money into US dollars and spend those US dollars on shares. On Sharesies, you pay a currency exchange fee when you make an exchange to buy foreign shares.

But just like shares, the value of currencies changes all the time. For example, if you changed NZ$100 into US dollars in December 2019, you'd have received around US$67. If you did the same exchange in March 2020, you'd have received US$56 — a reduction of $11. By September 2021, the New Zealand dollar had picked up again and would have bought US$71.50.

The same NZ$100 would buy fewer US shares in March 2020 than it did in December 2019, if those shares were worth the same amount of US dollars. But then by 2021, it would have bought more. This added level of fluctuation is something to take into account when you invest internationally.

It can work in your favour — and against you — in lots of ways.

Let's say you buy US shares using US dollars (USD) you've just converted from NZ dollars (NZD). Later, you might decide to sell those shares, and convert the USD back to NZD. If you convert when the US dollar is worth less than it was when you bought the shares, your NZD returns will be reduced.

The opposite can also happen. If you do that same conversion when the US dollar has become more valuable, then your NZD returns will be higher.

There are four different ways that the exchange rate can affect your investment. When you sell US shares, and convert the USD to NZD:

- If your investment has gained value, and the US dollar has gained value, you get a higher return.
- If your investment has gained value, and the US dollar has lost value, you lose some of your return.
- If your investment has lost value, and the US dollar has gained value, you lose less than what you would have otherwise lost.
- If your investment has lost value, and the US dollar has also lost value, you make even more of a loss.

On the one hand, foreign exchange movements can amplify your return. But on the other, it can make a loss worse.

Why do currency prices change?

Currency and shares are really similar. Both are traded on markets, and both have their prices set when buyers and sellers agree on a price, and make a trade.

This means that currencies change their price based on supply and demand. If lots of people want to buy a currency, and there aren't many people selling that currency, then the price will go up. Of course, the reverse is also true. If few people want a currency, and lots of people are trying to sell it, then the price will go down.

Whether people want a currency (and how much they'll pay for it) is driven by all kinds of things, like interest rates, economic prospects, demand for exports, money supply and inflation expectations.

Interest rates

If one country has high interest rates, while another country has low interest rates, then some people may want to borrow money from the country with the low interest rates and put it in a bank account in the country with the high interest rates. This increases demand for the second country's currency, and generally makes it more valuable. (In fact, it can balance out the difference in interest rates pretty quickly.) This has been seen in New Zealand and Australia in recent years — although interest rates have been low by historical standards, they haven't been as low as in some other countries, which has supported the Australian and New Zealand currencies.

Economic prospects

If a country has a booming economy, people from around the world will want to invest in that economy. To do so, they need to buy local currency — and when they all compete for local currency, the price of that currency goes up. This helps to keep currencies of big economies strong, like the US and the UK, particularly when they are seen as safe havens if there's a bit of turmoil going on elsewhere.

Demand for exports

If a country exports a lot more than it imports, then those exporters need to turn their foreign currency back into local currency in order to spend it. This increases demand for the country's currency, and pushes its price up (this happens in New Zealand and Australia, which both export lots of goods). But the opposite can also happen, and a currency can become less valuable if a country's exports become less valuable. Exporters don't tend to be big fans of their local currency increasing in value because it means the goods they export are worth comparatively less.

Money supply

The more money there is in the economy, the easier it is to get hold of. A country that is printing lots of money will sometimes have a lower exchange rate than a country that is not printing very much money. You might have heard about money printing around the world as the effects of Covid-19 were felt on economies.

Inflation expectations

Inflation causes a currency to become less valuable. The fact that a can of Coke costs more than double what it did about 20 years ago is an example of inflation. If people expect inflation to be high, and for a currency to lose value in the future, then they won't want that currency today — which will in turn cause it to lose value. This matters when one country is going through a period of higher inflation than others.

How to manage foreign-exchange risk

Every investment has risks and opportunities, and exchange rates are just another risk (and opportunity) to understand and manage. Just like shares, there are three ways to manage the risk of exchange rates moving around: diversification, having a long time horizon and dollar-cost averaging.

Diversifying is a matter of owning investments in both foreign currencies and your own dollars. That way, shifts in relative exchange rates get balanced out. If you own US shares and local shares, and the exchange rate moves, then one of your currencies gains value while the other loses value. The movements cancel one another out if they're similar amounts of each currency. If you invest via a fund, the manager considers this for you.

The other way you can manage foreign-exchange risk is by having a long time horizon (is all of this sounding familiar?). Foreign currencies tend to move around a lot day to day and week to week, but also tend to be reasonably stable over five years, 10 years, or more. If you know you're investing for a period of many years, you won't worry so much about what the currencies you're investing in are doing right now.

Remember our old mate dollar-cost averaging, which meant that you wouldn't need to overly worry about the price you paid for your various shares?

Dollar-cost averaging (where you invest on a regular basis, rather than all at once), also protects you from the swings in foreign exchange rates. If you invest every week or month, you might get stung by a low exchange rate sometimes, but also get the benefits of a high exchange rate at other times. This approach also applies when selling investments. Combine this with diversification and a long time horizon, and it balances out.

Foreign exchange can amplify gains and losses, so it's worth considering when you're investing overseas. But, like all risks, it's a risk that you can manage over time. Bear it in mind, think about how you're going to manage it, but don't let it stop you from investing.

Dual-listed companies

Every so often, you will come across a company being described as 'dual listed'. This means that its shares trade on two different stock exchanges — often, when we talk about dual-listed companies, we mean that a company is listed on both the New Zealand stock exchange (NZX) and Australian stock exchange (ASX).

Why? First, it's generally easier for investors to invest in companies that are listed on their home country's exchange.

If a company wants its shares to be available to a wider range of potential investors, it makes sense for it to list in more than one country. That's why some NZ companies list on both the NZX and the ASX. Listing on the ASX makes it easier for Australian investors to buy and sell their shares, and to turn their shares into cash.

Access to a broader and more diverse group of investors also gives the share price more price support because there are larger numbers of investors willing to pay a certain amount for those shares. More price support from a broad range of investors can give a clearer view of what the market thinks a company is worth. The share price isn't as reliant on a small group of investors who might be swayed by other factors.

Dual listing could also make it easier for a company to raise cash. With access to a greater pool of prospective investors, they can raise a lower amount of money from each investor to meet their funding goals.

What does dual listing mean for investors?

Generally, it's easier and cheaper to invest in companies on local exchanges than it is to invest in companies on overseas exchanges. You don't have to worry about foreign exchange and you don't need to think about whether there are any tax implications.

Investor story: offshore investing

Hadleigh had a few friends who were already investing in Sharesies when he began in 2018, and they seemed to be making good returns from their investments.

'I was also aware that rich people don't tend to just leave their money lying around in the bank,' he said. 'They often seem to invest it, buy themselves assets and so forth. I kept that in mind and decided I wanted to do that, too, but I didn't know where to begin. Then I heard about Sharesies.'

After reading a positive review, he decided to give it a go with an initial $3000 investment. 'I sort of just started experimenting with that.'

He invested in some exchange-traded funds, and bought shares in a couple of American companies that he was interested in, such as Tesla, Inc. (NASDAQ:TSLA). 'My logic was that any profit is good profit. I'm not greedy but I do want to protect my money. I was quite happy to diversify my investments by buying ETFs from different regions of the world and different industries, so I would be insulated from any kind of dips in a particular market.

'That's worked out really well for me. When we had that big dip when the pandemic began, it didn't affect me too much. The only way it affected me was that I bought a whole lot of extra stock for really cheap at the time and I'm glad I did.'

Hadleigh plans to hold on to all of his investments for now. 'I don't really buy and sell very often. I just buy and every now and then I'll sell. I normally only sell something in order to buy something I like more.'

He has an auto-invest set up every week that buys units in five ETFs. 'That just sits there, slowly building up. Over time I see it growing. I also regularly put extra money in other individual companies. They might be technology companies, or those that are involved in things I think will be important in the future,' he says.

'I see sustainability as being important because we have a finite amount of resources on the planet and companies that are responsible seem like a wise investment to me. Things like water care — we're always going to need water but there's a finite amount of water and you have to look after it. I think it's worth investing in things that are positively shaping the future of our civilisation.

'The way I see it, even if I do lose some money it's not the end of the world because I'm investing in the future I want to see. I can feel glad I'm putting my money towards creating that future and effecting positive change in the world. That being said, I haven't lost any money doing that.

'I buy them when I feel like it, when I've got the money or I see a dip in the market, otherwise I have my auto-invest ticking over in the background.'

Hadleigh says he thinks of his investments as 'spicy savings' or like KiwiSaver with a bit more control.

'I'm a bachelor with no debt, I have a reasonable amount of disposable income. I don't really get a kick out of going down to the mall and buying shoes or cars or things that will depreciate. What I do get a kick out of is buying companies and literally owning part of a company I believe is going to grow — then watching it happen.'

Hadleigh says the Sharesies experience makes it feel like he is shopping, even though he isn't. 'I just bought $100 of something and it will give me the same kick I'd get from going to the mall but I have something to show for it rather than a pair of shoes. Whenever I get paid, I transfer a bit over to my Sharesies wallet and play around with it, buy whatever I'm into at the time. There are a few companies I feel a high level of conviction about and I keep investing in those companies. I've had a really positive experience — I've doubled my money.'

Being an investor had motivated him to learn more about the economy and how the stock market worked, he said. 'I intend to continue investing with the ultimate goal of selling when I have enough money for a deposit for a house. That's a longer-term goal.'

Hadleigh sets aside his own savings in a separate bank account and said he had more money in there than his Sharesies account.

'The money in my bank account has made me very little money compared to my investments. If I had gone all in with Sharesies at the beginning I would have more money than if I left it in the bank, depreciating with inflation.'

What now?

- Check your investment portfolio. How diversified is it? Is most of your money invested in one country?
- Consider your investment goals. Where might you find other investment opportunities that could be in line with your goals or values?
- Are there any companies around the world that you're particularly excited about, and want to get involved with?
- Are there any companies or technologies you use every day that you think everybody else should be into, too?
- Check out the options on Sharesies. If you're keen on getting a slice of an international market, would funds or a

direct investment be a better option?

- Do your due diligence on anything you're considering. Why is it a good investment for you? What do you expect to see it do in the future?
- Keep up to date with what's happening in the markets you're invested in. Remember not all the international financial news makes it to your local media, so you may need to actively look for the coverage you want to find.

6.

Impact investing: how to make a difference

Y ou'll know by now that when you invest, you're doing more than just making a decision on how to get the best return on your cash.

Whether you're putting your money directly into companies on the sharemarket, or investing your money in funds, you're backing the things that you believe will have a great future — and helping to shape the future for all of us. Even when you're not giving it any active thought, your investment dollars can be working hard.

What if you want to take it further, and really make sure that you do everything you can to make the change you want to see in the world, with every investment in line with your own personal beliefs and values?

The idea of voting with your money is not new — investors have for centuries avoided putting their money and other resources into investments they didn't agree with. But over recent years, there has been a big increase in more formalised 'responsible' or 'impact' investing.

There are a few ways that investment managers talk about doing this.

You might hear people refer to social and responsible investments, which means that a fund decides not to invest in 'unacceptable' industries, such as tobacco or fossil fuels.

You might have also heard of impact investing, which refers to investments made with the intention of generating a positive change — usually social or environmental.

You might say you're following a responsible investment strategy if you avoided anything that invested in fossil fuels, for example. Or you might put your impact investing strategy into action by voting with your dollars and only backing companies that have good gender diversity in their upper levels. You might want to ensure that you invest in line with your vegan philosophy.

People are into things like clean energy, and backing companies such as Tesla, Inc. (NASDAQ:TSLA) that they see to be leading the charge (no pun intended). They clearly want their investment portfolios to reflect the things they value in their day-to-day lives.

But what is considered important varies a lot from one investor to another. Some are driven by religious considerations, some are more worried about social outcomes and some care most about the environmental impacts of their decisions. There's a big spectrum — you might not like the idea of investing in alcohol companies, for example, while your friend is comfortable with that but doesn't like the idea of gambling software.

That means, when it comes to responsible or impact investing, we can't give you any clear rules on what you should do or how you should do it. But we can offer you a guide on where to begin. It's also worth remembering that any investment strategy you pick does have risks, so the same guidance of how to be aware of and manage these risks that we cover in Chapter 2 applies to when you're considering the impact of your investments, too.

How to be an impact investor

Your first step should be to consider the outcome you would like to see.

What's most important to you, and how do you want your investment portfolio to address that?

Your ethics are personal to you. There's no absolute right or wrong answer as to which investments are ethically acceptable, and which investments are not. Different people value different things and that's OK.

But if you want ethics to be part of how you make investment decisions, you should think about which issues matter the most to you. Are you concerned about climate change? Do you care about equality and inclusion? What about workplace health and safety, or workers' rights in general?

It might be useful to write a list on some paper. Organise the things you care about under a traffic-light system — the red issues are the issues you don't want your investments to touch at all, while the green issues are things you actively want to invest in. Everything in the middle is an orange issue, which you can decide on a case-by-case basis.

Your money can make a big difference. The more people who invest for the world they want to see, with whatever they can afford, the bigger the impact.

Once you've got your priorities clear, you can start mapping these issues to different investments. If climate change was one of your red issues, then you may not want to invest in an oil company.

If gambling was one of your red issues, then a casino may not be the investment for you.

But this is easier for some issues than it is for others. If you're really concerned about human rights and workers' rights, how do you figure out which organisations are treating their employees well, and which ones aren't? What's more, how do you define something like that in the first place? This will require a bit more investigation (more on that in a minute).

Managed funds

Managed funds are a great way to invest responsibly, because many funds make doing exactly that their number one priority and take care of all of the research. You'll usually be able to spot these funds because they refer to themselves as 'responsible', 'ethical' or 'social'.

If you find a fund that shares your values or investing ethos, and matches your strategy and goals, then it's worth exploring further and seeing if it's the right one for you.

Managed funds all have a fund manager that manages them (the job title might give it away). The manager then has a certain mandate that they work towards. Depending on whether they're actively or passively managed, they'll be reviewing investments to make sure that they live up to the description on the fund's proverbial tin.

Funds all have a product disclosure statement (PDS) or prospectus that you can read to get a sense of what they are trying to achieve. It may also detail their top 10 holdings to give you an idea of how they are accomplishing it. You can also check out the fund manager's website for an in-depth look.

You might see reference to funds following an ESG strategy.

ESG stands for Environmental, Social and Governance. Funds that follow an ESG strategy, sometimes referred to as a Responsible Investment Strategy, will make investment decisions on how well companies perform against their expectations of what ESG means. The fund might consider how companies treat the environment, First Nations engagement, treat local communities and their employees, as well as a bunch of other considerations. Fund managers are likely to have their approach to ESG investing published on their website, so visiting their site to review their responsible investment policies may give you a better understanding of how they've made their decisions.

The benefit of investing in funds that have a strategy for approaching ESG, is that they conduct research into companies that fit within their ESG strategy, which may reduce your workload to find which investments align to your values.

But there are a couple of trade-offs as well:

- While you might occasionally find a perfect fit, often your values probably won't 100 per cent align with the way the fund applies ESG principles.
- There's no standard set of rules for what makes a company 'good' or 'bad' in terms of ESG. So it's worth researching the fund, to see if they've published an ESG strategy. Do they seek out 'good' investments, or do they just avoid 'bad' ones? How do they define ESG criteria? The closer these definitions are to your own set of values, the better.
- The important thing to remember is that there's a broad spectrum of ESG approaches — so if this is important to you, get a good handle on how the funds you're investing in apply ESG.

Exchange-traded funds (ETFs)

ESG information isn't as easily accessible for exchange-traded funds and there is a lot of variation between the different funds. You can read the description of the fund, see what it invests in and work out whether it's a good fit for you.

Google will also be your friend if you want to find out more. Some ETFs follow a specific theme, such as responsible investment or ethical investment, or a sector such as robotics. The Smartshares Europe Equities ESG ETF Fund (NZX:EUG), for example, invests in 400 European companies but screens out any investment in thermal coal, oil sands, controversial and nuclear weapons, firearms and tobacco. The Global Equities ESG Fund invests in 1500 companies from around the world with an ESG strategy, screening out the same sorts of things as the Europe fund, and excluding companies that violate the principles of the UN Global Compact.

You can look at the holdings of ETFs to ensure that you are putting your money into funds you are comfortable with. As the holdings in the ETF might change, what is included in an ETF now won't necessarily be the same in a year's time. If an ETF isn't explicitly screening for particular concerns, you might want to check in regularly to make sure it hasn't picked up any companies you are concerned about.

Companies

If you want to pick the specific companies to put your money into, creating your own portfolio may be the best way to make this happen. To do this, just go through the red, orange and green light exercise you did earlier, and figure out which companies sit within each colour.

Then, you can use that information to drive your investment decisions.

You can google a potential investment with some key words related to issues you care about. Are news stories coming up that you don't like the look of? Conversely, are you hearing reports that really resonate with you? Remember, ethical investing isn't just about avoiding investments that are getting things wrong, it's also about supporting investments that are getting them right.

You can also go deeper if you want. Some companies release specific reports into sustainability and other ethical issues. You can read these if they're available, and use the information in them to make a decision. Otherwise, you can just look through annual reports, as these give a pretty good idea of what companies care about, and what they invest their money in.

If you can, look for an integrated annual report, which covers not just the financial aspects of the business's performance but the non-financial, such as its impacts on the community, economy, environment and wider society.

If you want to do an extra dig, you can check out the key players in the company. What's the CEO known for? It's now common for business leaders to have blogs, podcasts or TED talks that will give you a bit of an insight into how they operate, and a feel for the company.

Of course, the trade-off here is the time it takes to research each company in your diversified portfolio of investments. As with everything in ethical investing, it's up to you and how you want to express your particular values.

You can also look for accreditations — whether a company is a B Corp, for example (more on that in a minute) or has any of the carbon neutrality or living wage marks.

Have a look and see whether companies are being held accountable to the claims that they are making — is the board asking for reporting on emissions? Are they auditing for a gender pay gap?

Adding or avoiding?

Sometimes, responsible investment managers will surprise you by holding on to investments in companies that you might think are not a great fit with their mandate — maybe something like a really heavy carbon consumer.

There are two main schools of thought when it comes to making a difference with investment. Some people think you should just avoid anything that doesn't work with your philosophy. But others think that some of these companies need resources (and advocacy) to make the changes they need, and that remaining invested but lobbying for what you want to see is more effective. There have been some pretty fiery AGMs recently, where investors have been doing exactly that.

Sometimes making a shift to renewable energy, say, is really expensive and would not be possible for a company if investors all bailed. But if the investors maintain support, a big company can make a really impactful switch. If you see a fund holding an investment that concerns you, find out why it's there. Is the fund manager working as a shareholder activist to drive change?

In New Zealand, it's common for funds, particularly super-annuation funds, to avoid tobacco and controversial weapons, like landmines, cluster bombs and nuclear weapons.

But a Mindful Money survey[14] showed that New Zealanders

---

14 'Mindful Money Methodology: Avoiding Issues of Concern', Mindful Money (website),https://mindfulmoney.nz/news/entry/mindful_money_methodology/

were also worried about investing in funds with exposure to gambling, pornography, alcohol, fossil fuels, other weapons, palm oil, human rights violations, environmental damage, genetic modification and animal welfare.

It's possible to find funds that exclude these concerns, too.

Mindful Money notes that fund managers dropping stocks because of concerns about them have usually looked to get rid of things on moral or religious grounds. Mindful Money founder Barry Coates notes that we've seen trillions of dollars' worth of assets divested from fossil fuel producers internationally, as well as campaigns to avoid investing in tobacco, nuclear weapons and cluster munitions. He says that these divestment campaigns have been effective in de-legitimising companies and achieving change, as well as allowing investors to avoid harm by excluding companies that do not align with their values.

Some funds meet their mandate by screening for anything they do not think is appropriate — basically just excluding that from their investment portfolio. A manager might have screens for tobacco, fossil fuels, alcohol or weapons. This works but critics say it can be an inflexible way of meeting a mandate and doesn't necessarily target change.

Other funds, though, invest by looking for the top performers in an area and making sure they are included. Coates says many of the actively managed investment funds also invest more of their portfolio in companies with better standards — those that have higher ESG scores and a more positive impact. This can have a significant effect on demand for higher-impact companies, as has been seen in the rapid share price increases for renewable energy producers.

How common is a desire to invest responsibly?

If you're in New Zealand, you may remember this story. But wherever you are in the world, it's an interesting anecdote about the power of investigating where your money is going.

In 2015, a series of media reports about what KiwiSaver (superannuation) funds were 'really involved in' generated headlines that seriously shocked some investors. Some people found out that their retirement savings were in companies that were making things they were really opposed to — like munitions.[15]

Over the next year, managers hurried to get out of any exposure to companies making cluster bombs, landmines and nuclear weapons, and tobacco companies as well. Over the course of 12 months, there was a 67 per cent increase[16] in the number of 'responsibly' managed funds in the KiwiSaver sector even though most funds only made small changes.

This could be viewed as one of the biggest and fastest shifts in the world to responsible investing. By 2019, the Responsible Investment Association Australasia (RIAA) was saying that New Zealand had the highest proportion of commitments to responsible and ethical investment of any major global market.[17]

The pressure from the public and the media meant that managers had no choice but to act. As time went by, even more focus was put on the responsible investment options being offered.

15　'KiwiSaver, cluster bombs, mines and nukes', Stuff (website), https://www.stuff.co.nz/business/71324537/kiwisaver-cluster-bombs-mines-and-nukes

16　'Responsible investing and the art of KiwiSaving the Planet', Stuff (website), https://www.stuff.co.nz/business/money/98353190/responsible-investing-and-the-art-of-kiwisaving-the-planet

17　'New Zealand a market leader in ethical investment – report', RNZ (website), https://www.rnz.co.nz/news/business/393955/new-zealand-a-market-leader-in-ethical-investment-report

There was criticism that those managers who responded to the initial cluster-bomb push were giving no thought to how they could influence companies to implement better ESG practices. Later developments have seen more nuanced KiwiSaver responsible investment strategies developed.

Responsible investment is growing in popularity around the world and it's become increasingly obvious that the way we invest — and the way our companies perform — has a huge impact on the rest of us.

Responsible investment is no longer niche but mainstream — investors now expect that they won't be surprised with an investment in something they find abhorrent.

As more retail investors have started investing through accessible platforms like Sharesies, they've been able to invest in the future they want to see. We can act and react on the information we have to hand — we don't have to wait to amass a lump sum to invest via a traditional broker.

RIAA reports on the uptake of responsible investment on both sides of the Tasman

RIAA's 2021 report showed the amount of money in responsibly invested funds in Australia increased by A$298 billion to $1281 billion in 2020.[18]

The amount of money invested with the rest of the market dropped by A$234 billion to A$1918 billion.

The proportion of responsible investment assets under

18 'Responsible Investment Benchmark Report Australia 2021', RIAA (website), https://responsibleinvestment.org/wp-content/uploads/2021/09/Responsible-Investment-Benchmark-Report-Australia-2021.pdf

management to total managed funds in Australia was 40 per cent in December 2020, compared to 31 per cent in 2019.

In New Zealand, there was NZ$142 billion in responsibly managed funds in 2020, or 43 per cent of total funds under management, up from 38 per cent in 2019.[19]

RIAA said 25 per cent of consumers wanted to avoid fossil fuels and 15 per cent wanted to avoid companies that committed human rights abuses. But fund managers were most likely to avoid tobacco (22 per cent), fossil fuels (16 per cent) and weapons and firearms (15 per cent).

It conducted research with Mindful Money that showed that two thirds of the people spoken to planned to invest ethically within the next five years, and most of those within the next year. A total of 60 per cent said they would be motivated to save and invest more money if doing so would make a positive difference to the environment and society.[20]

Case study: Tahito

There are many funds that apply ESG principles in their approach to investing. You can find the information to support how a fund takes into consideration ESG sustainability and ethical values by looking at their websites and disclosures.

---

19 'Responsible Investment Benchmark Report Aotearoa New Zealand 2021', RIAA (website), https://responsibleinvestment.org/wp-content/uploads/2021/09/Responsible-Investment-Benchmark-Report-Aotearoa-New-Zealand-2021.pdf

20 'Media release: Consumers on the money with ethical investing', RIAA (website), https://responsibleinvestment.org/wp-content/uploads/2020/10/Media-release-NZ-consumer-research-FINAL.pdf

One such fund is the TAHITO Te Tai o Rehua Fund (Tahito), a New Zealand-based fund. This case study is not intended as an endorsement or promotion of Tahito. Always review a product's disclosure documents before making a financial decision to ensure it meets your objectives and personal circumstances.

Fund manager Tahito launched in 2019 with its first fund, the TAHITO Te Tai o Rehua Fund.

It takes an ethical and sustainable approach to investing and measures companies based on Māori ancestral knowledge. It integrates MCSI (Morgan Stanley Capital International) environmental, social and governance research into that screening and takes a long-term view.

It considers things like whakapapa (holistic connection to the world we live in), aroha (relational connections) and mauri (life force). It invests in high-quality companies that it sees displaying connectivity and relational behaviours, with a commitment to a low environmental impact and a high level of social and corporate responsibility.

At the end of June 2021, its Te Tai o Rehua Fund had returned 14.4 per cent a year since inception.

In June 2021 we talked to Temuera Hall, Tahito co-founder and managing director.

WHY WAS TAHITO STARTED?

Tahito started from the meeting of minds and the blending of worlds. We had the conviction that a Māori-indigenous, ethical, and sustainable-based offering would appeal to a growing portion of the community.

Myself and my long-time friend and colleague, Chris Winitana, are the architects of Tahito. The Investment Services Group (ISG) were keen to support this innovative approach as they embarked on their sustainability journey. After two years of research and development in partnership with ISG, Tahito Limited was established.

While we were comfortable with our respective finance and investment knowledge, and cultural wisdom, we acknowledged that we were on an innovative journey into new territory — to blend the Māori world with the world of finance.

We're applying our ancestral Māori knowledge to benefit future generations. We want to leave a better world for our tamariki (children) and mokopuna (grandchildren).

HOW DOES TAHITO DIFFER FROM OTHER MANAGED FUNDS?

Tahito is a unique way of measuring companies using Māori ancestral knowledge, environmental, social, and governance (ESG) data capture technology, and strong financial analysis. Companies in the fund need to meet rigorous requirements such as no fossil fuels, a low carbon footprint, no armaments, diversity in governance and senior management, and a high ESG quality. [We use] positive investment screening: our screening process has over 50 quantitative and qualitative measures to ensure your investment is applied ethically and sustainably with positive social and environmental purpose.

Negative business involvement screens are conducted to ensure alignment to our ethics and to check that we haven't missed any non-compliant business activities in the positive screening process. The fund has outperformed its market index to date (past performance does not guarantee future returns).

The Tahito investment team backs its decisions with robust and thorough financial analysis, research, and portfolio construction with a focus on long-term, sustainable growth and resilience. Tahito, its products and services, are part of the Investment Services Group.

As some sectors have few to no investments that meet our ethical and sustainability threshold (like the resource or industrial sector), we may experience periods of underperformance when these sectors perform well (mining is a good example). However, with our sustainability bias and disciplined approach to risk management, we aim to outperform the broader trans-Tasman index over the long term.

WHAT DOES ETHICAL INVESTING MEAN TO TAHITO?

The Māori worldview is relational and interconnected, and its foundation is captured in whakapapa (genealogy). Whakapapa maps connection: 'Everything is interrelated, nothing exists of itself.'

Māori ethics put people and the environment first because both are fundamental to living and thriving. This thinking falls out of the ancestral Māori worldview which centres on connection and the interdependence of all things. The Māori worldview ultimately follows nature's models. Its ethics strive for balance and consensuality, its behaviour is complementary and co-operational, its target is reciprocity and harmony.

WHAT KINDS OF ETHICAL SCREENS DO YOU DERIVE FROM MĀORI VALUES?

In applying our indigenous ethical lens, we're looking for behavioural qualities in companies that align with the value statements we've derived from our traditional knowledge:

- Whanaungatanga (tō ao) — Relational (display connectivity and value relationships)

- Whakapapa (tō mana) — Interdependent (serious about ethics and values)
- Whakarongo (tō hiwa) — Balanced (hold people and environment in high priority)
- Whakatau (tō kaha) — Consensual (open and transparent)
- Honotahi (tō wairua) — Complementary (equity, sharing wealth)
- Utu (tō mauri) — Reciprocal (care for and give back to the local communities)
- Mahitahi (tō tapu) — Co-operational (strong, competent leaders with a high awareness)
- Hūmārie (tō mārama) — Harmony (willing to compromise, adapt and engage new ideas)
- Kawa (tō ora) — Cyclical (long-term intergenerational and sustainable growth potential)

The investment process that underpins Tahito is effectively measuring aroha connection. By increasing your aroha (your level of connectivity), you increase your mauri (or life force), and we are on track to making the world a better place.

We're measuring the transition of companies from the substantive (internally focused, very self-absorbed behaviours), to the ideal relational (externally connected, collective behaviours). We look for leadership with a high level of compassion and selflessness.

For example, under Whanaungatanga tō ao we are looking at the company values, their vision, mission, and purpose. Under Whakarongo tō hiwa we screen for women directors and women senior executive managers. Under Honotahi tō wairua we are measuring community engagement and support.

WHAT KIND OF IMPACT ARE YOU TRYING TO CREATE WITH TAHITO?

Our fund is a contribution towards a new global story of equity, sustainability, and diversity. By investing in the fund, people are choosing to direct their capital to support businesses that Tahito believes are more likely to achieve a positive social impact.

In order to achieve impactful social and economic purpose, you first need leadership with the right belief, compassion and behaviours. We define this as being leaders who believe that to create equity, environmental sustainability and regeneration we need to avoid further concentration of wealth and wealth polarisation, strive for a quantum shift in economics — prioritising community and environmental wellbeing over profit and are committed to 'a new story' of how we want the world to be.

The ideal is aspirational — we can only start a journey towards that destination, as did our tīpuna (ancestors) when navigating the Pacific by the stars.

As mentioned above, Tahito is just one of many funds that have applied an ESG approach to investing and are supplying their investors with the information they need to determine if the fund is right for them. If you're looking for a fund that applies an ESG approach to its company selections, always read through the fund's responsible investing documents and policies and the product disclosure statements — so you can check if that fund aligns to your values.

Being a B Corp

We talked earlier about investing in companies that have accreditations or marks such as B Corp. At Sharesies, we know a lot about the B Corp process, because we are one — and it's a big part of our company values. Internationally, some big names are, too, like Ben & Jerry's (Ben & Jerry's Homemade Holdings Inc.) and Allbirds (Allbirds, Inc. NASDAQ:BIRD)

All B Corp companies have demonstrated a desire to reduce inequality, lower the levels of poverty, create a healthier environment and build strong communities.

When we became B Corp certified, we had to meet really rigorous standards of social and environmental performance. It was hard work but it showed that we are really serious about our goals and purpose.

For Sharesies, being a B Corp keeps us accountable for the way we want to work, and the way we believe every business should operate.

If a company is a B Corp, it should give you an extra level of reassurance. The company is operating with broad considerations of its impact.

If you're investing in managed funds, another thing you can look out for is the UNPRI mark (United Nations Principles of Responsible Investing). This is a UN-supported international network of signatories who are working together to implement principles for responsible investment, which are a guide for incorporating ESG issues into investment practice.

It was launched after then-UN Secretary General Kofi Annan started a process with some of the world's biggest institutional investors. They developed the principles based on the idea that ESG issues could affect performance of investment portfolios and should be considered alongside other financial factors, if the investors were to properly fulfil their fiduciary duty to their clients.

UNPRI signatories agree to contribute to a more sustainable

global financial system. A number of Australian and New Zealand fund managers are signatories.

Returns

Have you heard the one about how you'll need to give up some of your investment returns if you want to make a difference with your money?

Good news — it's a total myth that if you want to invest responsibly, you have to give up some of the financial benefits of investing.

Think about it like this — a company that safeguards the environment, or strives to have a positive impact on the community, theoretically should have a better long-term future than one that is flying through, maximising the return from all resources without any consideration of the cost.

If you are investing in a company that is heavily involved in fossil fuels, for example, its future profit could eventually run out when those fossil fuels are not so readily available. An investment in a big oil company won't look so good if it has poor processes that mean it has to spend millions cleaning up a spill.

Companies that are successful because they are exploiting resources will only be able to keep that up for so long before things start to look a bit less rosy. Mindful Money data shows that over the 10 years to 2020, coal stocks, measured by the Dow Jones US Coal Total Return Index, dropped by an average of 28.5 per cent per year.[21] Oil and gas share prices were flat over a 10-year period but halved in the period after 2015. Meanwhile the overall S&P 500 rose

---

21 'Myth Busting: Fossil Fuel Divestment', Mindful Money
     (website),https://mindfulmoney.nz/news/entry/myth-busting/

by an annual average of 12.65 per cent.

Companies that are aware of social and environmental issues, and preparing for them, actively governing to reduce their impacts on the world, are better equipped for the changes they'll have to deal with and are likely to be better prepared to thrive in future. They won't be surprised by something that comes along and takes a big hit out of their profit — they'll have known it was coming and worked to already be on the right side of history.

Companies that are worried about their reputation and brand are also likely to be more successful. Shareholder value can be dependent on intangible assets like ethical performance.

There's been a lot of research that proves this point:

- In one Harvard Business School study that looked at returns over 20 years, it was found that companies with good sustainability practices — things like cutting their waste and pollution and improving their income through sustainability innovations — had average returns almost 5 per cent higher per year than those with poor sustainability. It found that $1 invested in 1993 would have grown to $28 by 2013 if it was invested in companies with good performance on material sustainability issues — but if that money had been put into firms with poor sustainability performance, it would have turned in to just $14.[22]
- RIAA's 2021 report showed that responsibly invested New

---

22 'Turning a Profit While Doing Good: Aligning Sustainability with Corporate Performance', Brookings, (website), https://www.brookings.edu/research/turning-a-profit-while-doing-good-aligning-sustainability-with-corporate-performance/

Zealand share funds had returned 18.5 per cent over a year, compared to 13.9 per cent for the NZX50 index. Over 10 years, they had returned 15.8 per cent a year compared to 14.7 per cent for the index.[23]

- Morgan Stanley research analysed 10,723 funds using data from research provider Morningstar and found sustainable funds could offer lower market risk.[24] In years of 'turbulent times' the sustainable funds had much smaller 'downward deviation' than traditional funds.

- Analysis by Bank of America Merrill Lynch showed higher returns from portfolios with high ESG ratings and much less downside risk and bankruptcies.[25]

- Deutsche Bank looked at more than 100 studies of sustainable investing and found that responsible investing was shown to have a positive impact in 77 per cent of them.[26]

- The RIAA and Mindful Money survey mentioned earlier found almost 80 per cent of consumers expected an ethical investment strategy would outperform over the long term.

23 'Responsible Investment Benchmark Report Australia 2021', RIAA (website), https://responsibleinvestment.org/wp-content/uploads/2021/09/Responsible-Investment-Benchmark-Report-Aotearoa-New-Zealand-2021.pdf
24 'Sustainable Investing's Competitive Advantages', Morgan Stanley (website), https://www.morganstanley.com/ideas/sustainable-investing-competitive-advantages
25 'The Investor Revolution', Harvard Business Review (website), https://hbr.org/2019/05/the-investor-revolution
26 'Sustainable Investing: Establishing Long-Term Value and Performance', SSRN (website), https://papers.ssrn.com/sol3/papers.cfm?abstract_id=2222740

Greenwashing?

You might have heard of 'greenwashing' — it's the term for companies that try to make what they're doing sound more environmentally friendly than it really is. You sometimes see that when a cosmetics company tries to make its bog-standard shower gel sound like it's made of the purest plants by getting 'natural' in the brand name.

Investing in a fund, there is a risk that a fund manager might oversell its responsible investment criteria and make you think you're getting something more in line with your values than you really are.

You might hear that a fund would never have more than 5 per cent of its investment in a company that manufactures cluster bombs, for example. But if you end up with just under 5 per cent of your investment in the world's biggest cluster-bomb maker, that might not seem so good.

Regulators on both sides of the Tasman have looked at this issue and are making it harder for fund managers to fudge the details.

The Financial Markets Authority in New Zealand released some guidance, noting that demand for 'integrated' products was growing — those that took into account non-financial factors as well as financial returns. It said it would be keeping an eye on financial product providers to make sure that the impression they created for investors was accurate. It was clear that managers couldn't mislead or make false claims, and would have to substantiate any that they did make and disclose their approach.[27]

---

27 'FMA sets expectations for issues of "green" and "responsible" investment products', FMA (website),https://www.fma.govt.nz/news-and-resources/media-releases/expectations-green-investment-products/

In Australia, ASIC (Australian Securities and Investments Commission) said things could get confusing when a product issuer was not clear about the standards used to assess whether a product was environmentally or socially responsible or if its green credentials were 'overstated'.[28]

It's becoming harder for managers to be less than transparent about their processes, but it's still good practice to check you know where your money is going and what a manager is doing with it.

Something that makes responsible investing tricky is that there is a fair amount of subjectivity — what's a deal breaker for one investor won't be for another.

You can try to avoid greenwashing by looking critically at the standards that the product provider has had to meet, and the information set out in their disclosure documents.

---

28 'What is "greenwashing" and what are its potential threats?', ASIC (website),https://asic.gov.au/about-asic/news-centre/articles/what-is-greenwashing-and-what-are-its-potential-threats/

Investor stories: Guided by a moral compass

Lily only has a small amount of money invested in Sharesies but says she's hoping that it will eventually help her to amass a nest egg for retirement.

She used to invest in Bonus Bonds but when that was no longer an option, her husband suggested Sharesies instead.

'He puts in a bit each month and encouraged me to do the same.'

Lily looks at an investment's five-year share price history on Sharesies and invests in companies that have a positive trend, but stays away from anything that looks like it could have a connection to weaponry or negative environmental impacts.

'If I found out a company I liked had a poor moral compass I'd get rid of any shares I had.'

She says it's hard to get a clear understanding of how some companies might fit with her investment philosophy. 'I just hope that companies I have chosen are OK.'

Lily says the environmental and social impacts of her investments are more important to her than the financial return.

Meanwhile, Adam got into Sharesies in 2017, when he was fresh out of university and earning $16 an hour.

'Basically, I thought, I'm never going to get ahead at this rate. I knew at the end of my internship I would get a pay rise but I didn't know how much. I wanted to make my money do something more.'

He was only earning a couple of percentage points of

interest in the bank and wondered what other options might be available.

A quick google showed him that there were investment platforms internationally — and he wondered about his local options. 'I came across Sharesies and signed up — now it's been four years.'

At the beginning Adam would transfer $10 a week into his Sharesies account but increased that amount over time. 'At its height I was probably putting in $200 a week. I was flatting with my partner and working nights and weekends, I didn't really have a huge amount to spend money on so I ended up saving it. I thought it was better to invest it with Sharesies — at that point I probably could only have earned about 1.5 per cent from the bank.'

Most of Adam's money has been put into ETFs, starting with the Smartshares NZ Top 50 funds (FNZ). 'I was looking around and it seemed like that made up most of the economy. I thought if all the New Zealand economy goes into a slump I'm probably in trouble anyway and if it's going well then I want to take advantage of that. As time went on I learnt a bit more about diversification.'

Before he and his partner bought their house, he also invested in a property fund to get some exposure to that asset class, and also has money in the US 500 (USF), Australian resources (ASR) and NZ bonds (NZB) as well as the Smartshares Global Equities ESG Fund (ESG).

He says his original plan was to buy and hold investments but he and his partner had to tap into their accounts to buy a house.

'Sharesies was a big chunk of that. He had $5000 and

had made about $500 returns in the two years and I had put in $10,000 and had about $12,000. It had given us both a chunk of cash towards the house. We ended up selling 95 per cent of what we had.'

Now that they are homeowners, Adam is investing weekly again — 'but not as much as I used to'.

His goal is to have the sum in Sharesies grow large enough that he can clear his student loan, which was at $60,000 plus postgraduate study.

'I'm hoping Sharesies is going to help me — after that I'll look at financial independence.'

He said it was important for investors to know that they didn't need to pick the best investment and get it right the first time.

'The beautiful part of Sharesies is that you can invest small amounts often. If you're broad-based with something like an ETF, it doesn't really matter which specifics you pick as long as you pick something with a good track record that's broad enough to tick along with the economy. The wonders of compounding kick in after a couple of years.'

What now?

- Consider what's important to you. What's non-negotiable? What are your priorities?
- Work out how your current portfolio fits with that. Are you happy with the investments you've already chosen?
- Consider the risks associated with the company you're thinking about investing in. Are these risks within your risk appetite?

- Consider where you're going to put your money from here. Are there managed funds that are a good fit with your investment philosophy? Are there any companies that particularly appeal as investments?
- Are any companies doing social or environmental work that you really want to support?
- Get researching. Dig through annual reports and other information about companies you're considering to find out whether they are conducting themselves in the way you'd want a business you own a slice of to perform.

7.

How to know when to sell

As you'll already have realised, a lot of our Sharesies investors are in it for the long term and typically 'buy and hold'. There are lots of benefits to holding investments for a long time (but again, it depends on your personal circumstance if that's what's right for you). For a lot of people, that means that selling isn't something they think about very often.

While buying investments you love and holding on to them while your wealth grows is great, every so often you'll encounter a situation when you realise that something isn't sitting comfortably in your portfolio anymore, and you decide to sell. Or maybe you just need the money.

Here are a few reasons why people might sell an investment, and one reason why they shouldn't.

You've reached your goal

While some of our investors are investing for the sake of building up their wealth and aiming for a better future, others are doing so with a really clear goal in mind.

Maybe they want to build up enough money to pay off their student loans, or they need some cash to go towards a house deposit.

It's a good idea to always have some sort of goal for your investments, whether it's something concrete, like a wedding, or just something a bit ephemeral, like a desire to improve your financial future and provide for your kids.

Your goal could even just be to commit to invest a certain amount for a period of time — or to get a particular level of return on your investment. Some investors set out with a plan to stick with it until they double their money. That is a pretty good target to aim for — and when you get there you might review your strategy and decide that you want to keep going!

If you've reached your goal, that's a great reason to consider selling your investments, or maybe just some of them.

You can use the money for whatever you had intended, then move on to working towards your next target — and maybe make it even more ambitious.

Your circumstances have changed

Your investments sometimes need to change as you go through life.

If you started investing when you were single, with a bit of disposable income to play with, it might have made a lot of sense to take on more risk and see what you could make of your money, and to continue riding the changes in share price to see where they end up.

But if you have children and end up with several people relying on you to keep the household financially afloat, you might be a bit more inclined to take the returns you've made and reassess your portfolio.

In those circumstances, you might decide to sell some of your riskier investments and diversify into lower-risk investment or cash to make sure you have enough on hand in case of an emergency or you need to draw on it sooner than you expect.

The investment has changed

Do your investments still make as much sense as they did the day you bought them?

Do you still see the same future growth prospects for the businesses, or demand for the products? Do you still believe in the people behind the business and their goals and vision?

If you do, and you'd still buy an investment at its current price if you didn't already hold it, then you probably should not sell it.

But if something fundamental has changed, and you now think the current share price or unit price is not a good deal to a new buyer, it makes sense to rethink that investment, and perhaps move your money elsewhere.

If a business has hit a big problem — maybe demand for its products is evaporating like the patronage of Blockbuster in the past decade, or it has a big problem with a new product line — it could alter the growth trajectory you see for your investment, and change your opinion on holding on for the ride.

Maybe management has done something you fundamentally oppose or new leadership has come in, pursuing a different direction. When you wouldn't be keen to snap up the investment at its current price on the open market, it may be time to rethink your holding.

You really need the money

The reality is that sometimes life gets in the way of all kinds of things, and your investment strategy is no exception. If you get an unexpected expense, you might think about selling some of your investments to cover it.

Don't feel bad if this happens. It could happen to anyone. But double-check that you're truly in an emergency situation. Sometimes it's tempting to turn to the money you know is there in your portfolio, even though you might be able to find other ways to cover the expense if you didn't have that option.

Not all unexpected expenses are urgent — if you can put it off for a bit, and save up the money you need over time instead of selling your shares, you may end up better off in the long run.

Using shares as a financial back-up option is risky because their value fluctuates and you can't guarantee they'll be at a high when you need the money.

This is a good reason to have an emergency or rainy day fund, so that when something comes up, you can use your emergency savings account before you crack into your shares.

Having said that, if you're at the end of your rope, then go ahead and sell some shares. There's no shame in having to change your plans when something unexpected happens — and your investment account will still be there, awaiting your return.

One reason why you probably shouldn't sell

If the value of the investment is falling and you're panicking, or everyone else seems to be saying they are getting out, we suggest taking a breath, and reviewing your investment strategy to understand what's happening in the market and decide what's right for you.

The sharemarket can have lots of ups and downs.

Locking in a loss is when you sell your shares for less than you paid for them. It's what tends to happen when people panic and let the concerns of others overtake their own opinions about the shares they hold.

If the fundamentals of your investments haven't changed — the future growth you can see for the companies or funds you're invested in, your beliefs about their value and your own goals and circumstances — it makes sense not to sell, even if the share price isn't looking as healthy as you would like.

Locking in a loss is a big cost of selling shares and it happens often — even to people who say their goal is to buy low and sell high.

Remember, it doesn't matter that the share price has fallen if you weren't going to sell anyway. If you own shares that are worth less than you paid for them, you haven't actually lost anything. But if you sell shares that are worth less than you paid for them, you're locking that loss in for good. If the shares go back up in value after you've sold, you don't get those gains.

Ask yourself two questions: 'Did I plan on selling today?' and 'Has something significantly changed with the investment that makes me think it won't be as valuable in the future?' If the answer is no, then there's no reason to panic and sell early, just because the investment rollercoaster took a dip.

You can see this by looking at the Smartshares NZ Top 50 ETF (FNZ) fund share price. In October 2018, it was worth around $2.70. Then there was a bit of a dip — in January 2019, a share was worth $2.48. Anyone who bought in October and sold in January would have lost 22 cents per share.

But then things turned around — that same investment was worth $3.58 by September 2021. Investors who hung on would have been well rewarded. One thing's for sure with markets — they will continue to go up and down!

Selling too early can mean you miss out on growth

Beginner investors may panic and sell when things take a dip — but they also might sell too early when things go up.

Missing out on growth is similar to locking in a loss, but it's a lot sneakier because you still feel like you're winning, even when you're costing yourself future returns.

Let's say you bought some shares for $100, with the intention of sitting on them for a year. After six months, they've done really well — now they're worth $150. You haven't reached your time goal, but you figure a 50 per cent gain is really good. So you sell. After all, you're not making a loss, right? There's no doubt that a 50 per cent return is much better than you could have got from a savings account.

But there is bad news — you might still miss out. What if the share price keeps going up, and six months after you sell, those shares are worth $175, or $200? This isn't that different from locking in a loss — you've 'lost' the potential to make a better return by selling earlier than you intended. (It's worth remembering that past performance isn't an indicator of future performance, and your investment could go down, too.)

That's why it's important to review your strategy and check it is still relevant to your goals and risk appetite and apply all the same checks to selling an investment that has been performing well, as you would to one performing poorly.

Why timing the market is hard

Everyone wants to 'buy low and sell high', right? But not many of us actually manage it.

Even investors who think they're savvy and can pick an undervalued stock and ride it to success sometimes get caught out and actually do the opposite.

One of the big weaknesses of 'buy low, sell high' as a strategy is that it's very hard to tell if you're actually buying low or selling high. After all, 'low' is relative; a share price is only 'low' if you eventually sell it for higher later.

Of course, there's no way of knowing ahead of time if a share is going to go up or down. This means that when you 'buy low', you're essentially making an educated guess. You're saying that you don't think an investment is going to get much lower in price. But you can't know this for sure.

No one can ever pick the bottom or the peak of the market until it's happened — and usually by the time you can see a recovery taking place, you've missed the big initial bounce and you're stuck trying to catch up.

Let's say there was a company that used to be $3 per share, but it's been dropping over the past month. Now it's $2 per share. If you buy now, would you be 'buying low'? Maybe. Maybe not. It could drop to $1 per share, or lower. Or it could turn around, and rise. You won't know until later on.

The same goes for selling high. Let's say you bought some of those shares for $2. After a month, they were worth $3. Then $3.50. That's quite a bit higher than what you paid for them, so is now a good time to sell? Again — maybe. They could go back down to $2, or keep on rising.

It's enough to make you tear your hair out. In order to

successfully buy low and sell high, you need to time the market — and timing the market is extremely difficult to successfully, consistently pull off, unless you have a crystal ball. Even the experts get this wrong.

There are some benefits to choosing a time horizon further into the future and trying your best to stick to it. If you invest your money for 10 years or more, you have a better shot at earning higher returns than if you invested for fewer than 10 years. You'll need to stick with it through some market movements in that time but it is a much simpler strategy than trying to time the market. Of course, you need to balance the risks of doing this and regularly reassess your personal objectives and your financial situation and needs.

How to spot a bubble

People like to talk about investment 'bubbles' — especially people who haven't been brave enough to invest themselves.

Whether it's high house prices, cryptocurrencies, tech stocks or even tulips, everyone's got a story about a bubble that either already has burst or they reckon is about to.

A bubble is hard to define but, in our world, it's an investment that has seen its price grow without any clear reason.

When you're investing, there is always some potential baked into the share price. You're not just paying what you think the company is worth right now but what you think it might be worth in the future.

Prices often rise quickly — a business might be on to something exciting and growing fast, or a new chief executive might come in with a really exciting plan for the company.

But we get into bubble territory when the price is beyond the point of potential, and where there is nothing to substantiate it. There's been no change in what is going on at a company, yet suddenly its share price has shot up.

When a 'bubble' is taking hold more generally you might see people worried about missing out and a sense of euphoria in the market, with an expectation that prices will keep going up and up forever — just because that's what has been happening so far.

Generally, you can tell when things are starting to get a bit bubbly when you pull up one of those excited people and ask them why the price is rising so fast. If they can't tell you, that's a bad sign.

If you're worried about being caught by a bubble, try to put yourself in the shoes of others who are paying the current price. What do they think they are getting for their money? Has there been a change in what's happening, or can they see some potential that you can't?

But remember there are many more bubbles being predicted than bursting — or even existing.

Sometimes the reasons for a price increase might not be super obvious but that doesn't mean there isn't one. Behind the scenes there might be a view that the company is ripe for a merger or acquisition, and that could increase the share price. Investors might see equities as a whole as a good option in a low interest rate, higher inflation environment. You just need to identify what information is driving the price of any investment higher, and decide whether you agree that it makes it more attractive.

FOMO isn't a good reason to get in on anything and if it seems that someone is investing just because everyone else is doing it, that's probably not a good reason to follow.

Don't get put off something that is still a fundamentally good idea because other people are telling you it's a bubble. Remember, people have talked about 'house price bubbles' for decades — and yet prices have held firm. Anyone who decided in 2005 that they were going to wait for that bubble to burst before buying a house would have been disappointed.

What about meme stocks?

You might have heard some discussion about 'meme stocks' lately — whether that's chat about GameStop Corporation (NYSE:GME) or AMC Entertainment holdings Inc. (NYSE:AMC).

In simple terms, meme stocks are shares that are increasing in price because there's lots of chat about them, usually online, and they've become a popular thing to invest in.

That could be for lots of reasons — there were many reports of traders wanting to 'punish' hedge funds for shorting GameStop by pushing its price up.

But fundamentally, nothing has changed in the value of the company, so the price rises have an element of risk. You could make money if other investors keep piling in and pushing the price up.

But you could equally lose, if others realise that there's actually insufficient evidence that the value of the investment supports the price being asked.

Some platforms restricted trading in especially frothy meme stocks out of concerns that investors could get burned. But generally platforms won't stop you putting money into volatile investments but the orders can sometimes be delayed or rejected by the exchange.

Tulip mania[29]

Have you heard about tulip mania?

This seventeenth-century phenomenon is often cited as the earliest example of an asset bubble.

Tulips had not long been introduced to Europe and they quickly became a sought-after luxury item. As they became more popular, growers could ask for higher prices for the bulbs, which were sold on what were basically futures contracts to buyers who would promise to take them at the end of the season when the bulbs could be moved. (A futures contract is a legal agreement to buy or sell something at a set price at a specific point in the future.)

Growers soon discovered a variation that gave the flowers a multicoloured pattern, which became even more sought after and expensive.

Although it's hard to get clear price data, it's been reported that tulip bulbs were selling for about the price of a canal-front mansion, and about a million dollars in our modern currency, by the peak in 1636–37.

But then the value plummeted. People who bought bulbs on credit, hoping they could repay the loans by selling them on at a profit, were left stranded.

It might seem mad now to think about forking out hundreds of thousands of dollars for rare plants. Or maybe not, considering the price some variegated houseplants have recently commanded on online auction sites!

---

29 'Dutch Tulip Bulb Market Bubble', Investopedia (website), https://www.investopedia.com/terms/d/dutch_tulip_bulb_market_bubble.asp

What about when you don't get a choice?

Sometimes a company might delist from the stock exchange. This can occur voluntarily or not for the company, and it can have an effect on your shareholding. Set out below is a general guide on some common reasons why companies delist and what may happen to your shareholding afterwards.

It doesn't meet the exchange's requirements

Exchanges set their own requirements. The rules are based on numerous things like a company's market capitalisation, structure, share price and reporting obligations. If a company fails to meet the relevant requirements, the exchange will notify it of the breach and may halt trading in the company's shares pending resolution of the breach. Depending on the exchange and the type of breach the shares may stay in trading halt until the breach is resolved or the company is delisted.

It's gone through a merger or acquisition

If a company you own shares in goes through a merger (where two companies combine), it may be delisted if it's not the 'dominant' company coming out of the merger.

If a company you own shares in goes through an acquisition (where it's bought by another company), and the acquiring company buys all of the existing shares, the original company will be delisted.

It's struggling financially

If a company is in financial trouble, it may have to go through a legal process to either close the business for good, or help prevent it from closing. Usually, going through any of these legal processes will likely result in the company being delisted.

New Zealand and Australian companies are put into liquidation, receivership or administration if they can't pay their creditors (the people they owe money to) amounts they owe when due for payment.

- Liquidation — once a company enters liquidation, it means it will permanently stop trading and will soon cease to exist. Its remaining assets (like money, property and inventory) are sold and used to pay its creditors and, if any surplus remains, its shareholders.
- Receivership — a person is appointed as a receiver to collect and sell the company's assets, so they can settle the amounts the company owes to the creditor who appointed the receiver. A company cannot voluntarily put itself in receivership. The receiver is usually appointed by a creditor which has a charge over the company's assets when the company has breached its obligations to that creditor.
- Administration — a person is appointed as an administrator to take control of the company's operations and finances, and (if possible) come up with a plan for the business's future. Sometimes the company will stabilise and continue to operate, and other times it will be put into liquidation. The company can voluntarily put itself into administration, or be involuntarily put into administration by a creditor.

For US companies, you usually see reference to Chapter 11 bankruptcy (reorganisation) and Chapter 7 bankruptcy (liquidation). Filing for Chapter 11 bankruptcy means the company is asking to sort out its debts so it can try to re-emerge as a healthier business. If granted by a US bankruptcy court, the company gets time to form a plan and make some changes to the business, in the hopes that it will prevent the company from filing Chapter 7 bankruptcy (where the company needs to liquidate and shut their doors for good).

Here's what happens if a company you invest in is delisted

There are three main outcomes when a company delists:

You continue to own your shares

If the delisting occurs and the company remains in existence (and your shares have not been sold/cancelled), you will continue to own shares except in a delisted company. This means your shares will likely be illiquid and harder to sell, unless the company were to relist in the future. Prior to the delisting, you can usually expect the company's share price to be volatile, as investors are unsure of the future of the company, particularly if it is due to an insolvency scenario. In some cases, the company will relist and you'll continue to be able to trade your shares on the relevant stock exchange.

You get compensation for your shares

Other times, your shares might be cancelled or sold, but you'll be offered something in return. In a merger or acquisition, companies generally acquire other companies using cash, shares, or both. So, you could be paid out for your shares, or have your existing shares converted into new shares in the acquiring (or newly made) company. The impact of this depends on the terms of the merger or acquisition deal, and the price you receive per share.

You might receive a premium price for your shares. For example, if an acquiring company wants to take over the company you've invested in, it could offer a high price to incentivise enough shareholders to sell their shares. On the other hand, you might receive a lower price for your shares if the company you've invested in is experiencing financial difficulties. For example, if the deal is to save the company from liquidation, the price might be heavily discounted.

You don't get compensation for your shares

Unfortunately, if the company goes under then your shares can become worth very little or even worthless. This is most likely to happen when the company you've invested in goes into liquidation. Once in liquidation, shareholders are last in line to receive payment (after customers, creditors and debtholders) and it's possible that the company won't be able to offer them anything.

No one has a crystal ball, so it can be hard to know what to do when a company you've invested in might delist. Often the company will go into a trading halt before it's delisted, meaning you can't sell your shares, and your only practical option is to wait and see what happens.

To stay in the loop with what your investments are doing, you can keep an eye out for official company announcements on the website of the exchange they're listed on.

Remember — delisting a company and receiving no compensation is still an unusual outcome. This is a worst-case scenario — you need to know it's possible, but don't let it scare you off investing.

What's the OTC market in the US?

Sometimes, when a US company delists, its shares can still be bought and sold on an over-the-counter (OTC) market. An OTC market oversees trades of unlisted investments so is essentially just an unregulated trading platform. For example, a company that doesn't meet the requirements of an exchange, like the New York Stock Exchange (NYSE), might still be able to trade on an OTC market. In New Zealand, the equivalent is the Unlisted Market.

An OTC market is significantly less transparent than trading on a recognised stock exchange. It's less regulated and prices aren't publicly disclosed until a trade is complete. That means it's a lot harder to get pricing information, so prices can be volatile, and sell orders might take longer to complete.

Sharesies doesn't facilitate buying shares on any OTC market. However, if a US company you invest in delists and begins trading on an OTC market, you have the option to sell your investment if you want to, through a broker that would support this.

There are different reasons why a company might be delisted from an exchange, and it can be hard to predict what will happen to your investment if it does. Keep an eye out for official announcements from the companies you invest in, so you can stay in the loop with how they're doing, and give yourself time to do some research if something happens that you're not familiar with.

Mistakes investors make

No one wants to be caught out. But over the years we've seen a lot of investors making mistakes that reduce their overall outcomes, and could have been avoided.

Some are just part of the learning process — it's natural that people will make a few mistakes when they first start investing.

But if you can learn from others, you might be able to avoid a few of them in your own portfolio.

Not enough, or too much, information

When it comes to information about investing, there's a bit of a sweet spot. On one end of the spectrum, you want to have enough information to feel confident. Otherwise, you're less likely to invest in the first place. Educate yourself on the basics, so you understand concepts like time horizons, diversification and how to get started.

But then there's the other end of the spectrum. Some new investors get stuck into reading all about their investments. Is the global economy going to go into a recession? Or is it going to boom? What about that trade war we keep hearing about? What about Brexit? There's an election coming in Australia or New Zealand — does that matter? And so on and on . . . and on.

When you're consuming heaps of information and trying to apply it to your investments, it can be really hard to separate the signal from the noise. After all, big brokerages and managed funds hire whole teams of people to do this, and they still get it wrong quite often. You can end up feeling immobilised by all the information flooding into your brain.

Read up on the basics but try not to scare yourself by reading every piece of news that relates to your investing. After all, if you have a long time horizon, today's news stories are unlikely to have much of an effect on your investment in 10 or 20 years (depending on what the story is, of course).

Waiting for the bargain that never comes

If you look at the ups and downs of the sharemarket, it's easy to see (in retrospect) where the best buying opportunities were. Wouldn't it be great to invest when shares are $1, and immediately have them shoot up in value to $3, $4 or more?

The problem with this is that bargains are very obvious in

hindsight, and very hard to find ahead of time — unless you have a crystal ball. You can end up waiting for the price of an investment to fall just a little more every day before you take the plunge. Next thing you know, it goes up, and you've missed your bargain!

Rather than trying to wait for bargains and time the market, it's much easier to invest the same amount, on a regular basis — also known as dollar-cost averaging (remember that?). This means that sometimes you buy when prices are high, and sometimes you buy when prices are low — over time, your purchase price averages out, and you don't have to worry about whether you got a bargain or not.

Forgetting about the magic of time

Some would-be investors avoid investing because they think you need to invest a lot of money. If you don't have a lot of money, why bother?

But remember that investing for the long term means you don't need a lot of money at once. Say you want to invest a total of $20,000. You may not have that kind of money sitting in your bank account! But if your time horizon is 20 years, and you intend on investing once a week, you only need to come up with $20 a week. That's a lot more manageable than saving up a $20,000 lump sum.

What's more, when you invest what you can afford, even if it is just a little bit each week, you may see the benefit of compound returns instead of holding off making any investment until you've saved the full amount you want to invest. That's when your initial investment makes a return, then those returns are reinvested and make a return as well. Eventually, you'll be making returns on your returns' returns.

The cool thing about compound returns is that anyone can get them — you don't need to have heaps of money, you just need to have time, and the more of it the better. So the longer you wait to invest, the more compound returns you give up, and the sooner you invest, the more compound returns you get if these investments go up.

Time is your most valuable asset. Just choose an affordable regular investment amount, a long time horizon, build a habit and stick to it. If you can do that, you'll be well on your way to avoiding the most common investor mistakes and building your financial future.

What's liquidity?

You might have heard people talk about how 'liquid' an investment is.

Liquidity is a measure of how easy it is to get out of an investment and get your money back. If it's fast and inexpensive to exit, then it's considered a liquid investment.

For example, the cash in your bank account is very liquid as it's ready to spend almost instantly. In comparison, a house is a fairly illiquid investment. To turn it into cash, you'd have to sell it, or get your bank to loan you money against it. Both those options will take time and cost money.

Think of liquidity as a spectrum. Every type of investment you can make sits somewhere on the liquidity scale.

Ultimately, it comes down to how easily a buyer and seller can come together and agree on a price for the trade. Here are some key things that can determine this:

Market size

The more people that want to buy and sell an investment at the same price, the faster and easier it is to make the trade. As a result, bigger markets are usually considered more liquid than smaller ones.

Even within a market, investments can have varying levels

of liquidity. For example, large, well-known companies that list on the NZX or ASX tend to have more people wanting to buy and sell their shares than smaller, lesser-known companies listed on the exchange. As a result, shares in the bigger companies are usually more liquid.

Who can access the investment?

The more accessible an investment is, the more liquid it's likely to be. Listed investments (such as shares in listed companies, or units in ETFs) are more liquid than unlisted investments (investments that aren't listed on an exchange — like an unlisted company or fund) because they can be easily bought and sold through an exchange. Unlisted investments are sometimes only accessible to certain types of investors (like institutional investors) or at certain times (like when a company or fund wants to raise capital). This can mean the investment is less liquid as it's harder to find buyers and sellers.

Accessibility can also be affected by affordability. A house that costs $5 million is inaccessible to a lot of people.

How readily available are prices?

It's much easier to sell an investment if the current market price is easy to find, as there's less deliberation between the buyer and seller to agree on a price. The market prices of listed companies and funds are readily accessible and updated frequently through the exchange they're listed on. So, when you place a sell order for this type of investment, you generally have an idea of the price range it will sell at.

Meanwhile, the price of illiquid investments can be very hard to find. If you own an unlisted investment, you can't check an exchange to find out its latest market price. Some illiquid investments (like property, or shares in an unlisted company) rely on valuation experts to figure out how much they're worth. These valuations might come at a cost, take time, and may only happen periodically (like every quarter, year, or for special circumstances). This means that these investors generally have to accept that they won't always have access to up-to-date pricing, and that the time taken to buy and sell shares might be impacted by whether the pricing info is current.

What are the risks of an illiquid investment?

Like most things to do with investing, there's no hard-and-fast rule to determine the level of liquidity you should look for. Liquidity is another layer of risk, and there are some specific risks associated with illiquid investments.

The main risk of an illiquid investment is that it can be hard to sell your investment to turn it back into cash quickly. In an emergency, this can make it difficult to access your funds straight away. And if you manage to sell it, the potential costs of the process can cut into returns you might have made (or even your original investment amount).

Before you invest in an illiquid investment, you might want to consider when and how you'll be able to sell the investment.

As pricing information can be hard to gather or infrequent for some illiquid investments, it could be more difficult to track how your investment is doing. This might not be an issue for those with a higher risk appetite, but can be an added uncertainty for those who like to stay in the loop with their investments.

Some illiquid investments are designed to be held for a long time because of the time and cost associated with selling them. If you were to sell your investment before the intended time period, you could be negatively impacted by this. Even if you are investing for the long term, there's always the chance that you'll lose some, or all, of the money you started with.

Like other high-risk investments, illiquid investments can sometimes offer investors a chance at higher returns in the long run. In the finance world, this can be called a liquidity premium, and it's usually built into the forecasted (predicted) returns of an investment.

Investor story: The ups and downs

Auckland teenager Mark became interested in investing when his economics teacher began talking about his own investments.

Marc says he'd been thinking about investing for about three months before he actually started. 'During the 2020 lockdown I was earning the wage subsidy from my job at a call centre — I was earning all that money but had nowhere to spend it. I thought about putting it into Sharesies because I wasn't earning any interest in the bank.'

He started off quite conservatively, investing in big names and companies that had a strong track record. 'I did invest in retirement villages, because with all the baby boomers retiring that was meant to go gang-busters. It didn't really, but it's been alright.'

He made a steady profit from his portfolio until Auckland went into another lockdown in January 2021, when his balance wobbled a bit. 'Before the second wave of Covid, I invested liberally in quite risky investments and I lost a fair bit of money on those. Now I'm back to banks and funds,' he says.

'I get paid fortnightly and that just saves up in my bank account then I invest a lump sum when I feel like it.'

Marc focuses on companies that are likely to grow the most, although he is relatively conservative, wary of the effect of Covid on the market. His group of friends is also interested in investing, and like to egg each other on.

'Even when we're losing money it helps us get more invested,' he says.

What now?

If you're wondering about selling some of your investments, run through a quick checklist:

- Have any of the fundamentals of the investment changed since you invested?
- Do you think that the investment is now overpriced compared to its prospects?
- Do you need the money?
- Have your own circumstances changed to the point where the investment is no longer a good fit?
- If you answer yes to some or all of these, then it may be worth selling up.
- But if you're just worried because everyone else is:
  - Think about what might be causing the current worry — is it going to last?
  - Check your time horizon — have you still got quite a while to go before you're planning to cash up?
  - Remind yourself why you invested in the first place. Is that reason still valid?

8.

How to cope with a downturn

Many investors, particularly new ones, spend a lot of time worrying about the prospect of a downturn. But guess what? A downturn in the market isn't always a bad thing when you're an investor.

If you know what to do when a downturn comes, you can actually use these periods to your advantage.

Part of investing in assets like shares and managed funds is accepting that you'll see your investments go up and down in value from time to time. Don't be too worried about that.

If you don't want to accept more risk, stick your money in a bank account. But if you want to try for a better return than bank deposit rates, that means you have to ride out some movement.

When you know why you've invested, and what your strategy is, you can have the confidence to stick with it and make the most of the opportunities that arise in challenging times. Besides, there are lots of people who have made their money in a market downturn.

What can we learn from the past?

Over the last 50 years, there's been a serious downturn in the market roughly every 10 years or so. It's normal, and just the market doing its thing.

Sometimes, you'll hear this talked about as a transition from a 'bull market' to a 'bear market', as was the case in March 2020, when a very long run of higher returns came to a halt as the Covid-19 pandemic spread around the world. (One definition of a bear market is when prices drop at least 20 per cent from their height.)

The Great Depression (the first big sharemarket crash ending the excesses of the roaring 1920s), the 1987 Black Monday Crash (the famous end of the champagne culture of the 1980s), the Dot-Com Bubble (caused by excessive speculation in internet companies in the late 1990s), and of course, the GFC (the Global Financial Crisis between mid-2007 and early 2009) are just a handful of the many ups and downs we've seen. What you'll notice from them all is that generally prices went on to not just recover but actually exceed their previous highs.

People talk about a market 'correction' when prices drop more than 10 per cent from their previous peak. You can expect to see this every 12 to 18 months or so.

A crash is more extreme — it's a correction that happens really dramatically over a short period of time across a lot of the market. Crashes can be caused by a variety of reasons triggering heightened emotions such as fear and panic, as people face economic factors they aren't sure how to deal with. The worry can be contagious and spread among other traders, which makes the crash worse.

When you look back through history, you can see long periods of one-way growth, rising share prices and house prices, risky speculation by traders, banks handing out home loans whether people could afford them or not, and international political swings and roundabouts. This is often followed by a recession; a period of temporary economic decline identified by a fall in GDP (gross domestic product) in two successive quarters, and a shrinking economy. Boom turns to bust — but then, in time, the boom returns.

What do you need to know about a downturn?

The first time you see your portfolio balance drop can be pretty scary. No one likes to lose money.

The most important thing to do is to remember not to fret. Unless you've borrowed lots of money to get into your investments and you need to sell in the very near future, then a market downturn shouldn't be too much of a worry. There is also help on hand if you're keen for some extra reassurance for what's right for your situation, through an independent financial advisor.

To get the upwards momentum you want to see carry your investment portfolio to future gains, you need to be prepared to see some of that downwards movement, too.

How to manage your biggest risk in a downturn — you

Quickly give yourself a financial check-up — do you desperately need the money from your investments right now? If you don't and you can afford to hang in there — then it's worth seeing if you can ride the downturn out.

But hanging in there isn't all that you can do.

If you are prepared, you can take advantage of a downturn, too. After all, if you were at the supermarket and saw that some of your favourite cereal was heavily reduced in price, you'd probably stock up, right?

The same theory applies in a market downturn. When prices drop, shares can be viewed as being 'on sale'. If you still believe in the companies or the funds you are thinking about investing in, the market may be giving you an opportunity to jump in at a bargain price.

When you do, you're in a great place to ride the eventual upturn. Many people who have done very well out of their sharemarket investments were able to buy at the point when others were getting out. Loading up then gives them an even bigger portfolio to make the most of an eventual upswing in value.

Fund manager advice

Paul Brownsey, head of investment strategy at fund manager Pathfinder Asset Management, recommends people 'take a deep breath, and go for a walk' when they see something happening on the markets that they don't like.

'See for yourself that out in the real world, companies are still doing their thing. Construction companies are still building. Electricity-generating companies are still generating electricity. Supermarkets are still selling food. Telecommunications companies are still charging you a monthly fee to use your phone. Most people are still paying their Netflix, Inc. (NASDAQ:NFLX) subscriptions. Just because sharemarkets are down, it doesn't mean your investment will end up at zero.'

He suggested people might think about it as if they were looking to buy a new iPhone for $1000.

'You go back to the store today and it now costs $800. How do you react? Mostly by saying "Awesome, I just saved $200!" What if you were looking to invest $1000 into Apple Inc. (NASDAQ:AAPL) shares last week. If those same shares now only cost $800, shouldn't your reaction be the same? It's still a very good company. If it's still making a similar amount of money as it was before, then it must be better value now.

'If you have extra money to invest, down markets are good. You'll get better long-term returns when you invest at lower levels.'

Downturn strategies

So how can you manage yourself during a downturn?

There are some things you can do to feel a bit better about your financial situation if you decide to ride it out.

Build up your other reserves, particularly your emergency fund

An emergency fund is just what it sounds like — money set aside for emergencies, such as getting sick for a long time or losing a job. It doesn't need to be a lot, just enough so you can get by without any income for a while. A good rule of thumb is to have three to six months' worth of income for your emergency fund, but be realistic about what is achievable, too. Having this money set aside is a great psychological boost during times when your investments aren't performing well. And if you get stuck with an unexpected expense, you won't be forced to sell your investments at a bad time.

Pick an amount that works for your budget and that you can regularly set aside. Build up your emergency fund to a level that covers your needs.

How's your superannuation?

Don't let saving for retirement fall by the wayside. Keep contributing as long as you can — if you don't need your retirement money for a long time, try to resist the urge to move your money to a more conservative fund. People who do this tend to lock in the losses they've suffered, which could leave them a lot worse off at retirement.

Focus on the number of shares you hold, not the return they've delivered

You can measure your investment progress by looking at the number of shares (or part of a share) you own in various companies, or the number of units in funds, rather than the price of those shares or units. This will show you how well the downturn is setting you up for future success. Assuming that your investments perform well, a higher number of shares or units has the potential to result in a higher return when they rebound. It's likely that during periods of market weakness, if you continue to invest, the number of shares you own will increase more quickly (as you're buying them at a cheaper price).

Support the companies you're invested in

The quickest way out of a downturn or recession is for consumer confidence to pick up. You can do your bit by voting with your spending dollar, as well as your investing dollar, and doing business with the companies you want to see succeed.

Automate your investments

Less is usually more when it comes to monitoring your investments during a downturn.

Markets have gone through downturns before, and have always found a way to bounce back over the long term. If your portfolio is invested in line with your strategy in good times, and you still believe the companies or investments are sound and your personal circumstances haven't changed, then stick to the plan in the tough times, too.

If you no longer believe that the reasons behind why you made an investment stand true in the current environment and in your view of the future, you might want to recalibrate your portfolio. But watch out for loss aversion (being more willing to take risks to avoid a loss, than to make a gain).

If you need a break from constantly checking your investments, you might want to set up auto-invest instead. It's a simple way to put into place the practice of dollar-cost averaging, where you regularly invest a particular amount regardless of the share price. You can set it up so your money goes out of your bank account and into the funds you want without you having to do anything. You'll thank yourself for this in future if the price picks up again.

Manage your debt

Don't let your debt get away from you. Get rid of any high-interest debt as quickly as you can if the wider economy is going through a soft patch. If you have a mortgage, make keeping up with the repayments a priority.

The people who do best in a downturn are those in a strong financial position who can take advantage of opportunities.

Inflation

You might have heard people talk about inflation, and it's an important thing to get your head around when you're investing. Basically, inflation refers to prices increasing. It's something that central banks keep an eye on when they are setting official cash rates.

The big problem with inflation is that the money you already have becomes worth less because its buying power drops. That's a problem for people who like to keep their money somewhere with a relatively low rate of return. In a bank account with a low interest rate, for example, you could actually end up with the purchasing power of your money going backwards.

There are only two ways to fight inflation: by spending your money on something useful, like rent, groceries or petrol (or lollies), or by investing it, putting it to work for you, and getting a return that beats inflation. Otherwise, it slowly but surely fades away.

Central banks like inflation to sit at a rate of about 2 per cent a year. If every year, prices go up by around 2 per cent, your money becomes 2 per cent less valuable. The things that cost a dollar a year ago would cost $1.02 now. Like all percentages, the increase compounds — so inflation adds up faster than you'd think.

This might change the way you think about investing. Lots of low-risk bank accounts pay interest rates of between 1 and 3 per cent. On the face of it, this might seem OK — 3 per cent isn't very high, but on the other hand, it's very low risk (and remember to check out risks and fees related to the specific amount you're looking at).

But you need to subtract inflation from your returns to get your real (inflation-adjusted) returns. If inflation is 2 per cent, and you make a 3 per cent return, then your actual returns are a measly 1 per cent. Yikes. And if you make a 1 per cent return with 2 per cent inflation, you're actually going backwards by 1 per cent. On paper it looks like you gained money, but in real terms you actually lost money.

Remember 2 per cent is just used as an example, and it's possible for inflation to run much higher than that.

Beating inflation by playing the long game

If you have a long time horizon, one strategy of addressing the risks of inflation would be to invest in higher-risk growth assets, like shares. There are a couple of reasons for this:

- Over a long time horizon, shares tend to grow in value, on average (depending on the investment). They may be up and down year to year, but average returns usually look pretty good. So even when you adjust for inflation, you can still walk away with a pretty solid return.
- Inflation is about the money you spend right now. If a bottle of milk is more expensive now than it was a year ago, that only affects you if you're buying the bottle of milk. Any money you have invested for the long term is essentially 'protected' from inflation until you sell and want to use the money.

This second point means that inflation is a great motivation to stay strong if things go down. Let's say you've had some money invested for a year, and it loses 2 per cent of its value and inflation is 2 per cent. If you sell, you're actually locking in a 4 per cent loss. That's twice as much as it looks like you lost. But if you hang in there, you can hide from inflation until your returns turn things around. If you end up with a 7 per cent average return per year, and inflation was an average of 2 per cent, you're still getting 5 per cent. That's really solid.

Since inflation tends to average on the low side over time, and long-term returns on shares tend to be on the higher side, the longer you stay invested, the more likely you'll beat inflation. And that's on top of any of the great returns you may get anyway!

Volatility

You'll often hear people talk about markets going through periods of market volatility, if prices are moving around a lot.

A volatile investment is one that frequently changes in value by large amounts — up one moment, down the next. This means the price of that company or fund may move rapidly. Most investments have some volatility, but some investments are more volatile than others.

One easy way to see volatility is to look at an investment's value over time on a line graph (like the ones you can see on Sharesies when you check out the price history of a company or fund). A price history that looks largely flat has very little volatility, while something that's more of a rollercoaster is very volatile. On Sharesies, investments are displayed with a risk level of one to seven. Investments rated one are not very volatile, and will probably only have a few ups and downs. Those rated five or higher can expect to see movements of as much as 10 per cent or more. Volatility is not necessarily good or bad, but it's good to be aware of it.

Volatile investments have some positive attributes, and some negative attributes. Here's one side of the story: less volatility means more consistency. If you invest in something that's not very volatile, then that investment is less likely to drop in value. If it does drop in value, it's unlikely to be by very much.

Here's the other side of the story: volatility goes in two

directions — up and down. This can be a bit nerve-racking when a share's value is going down, but it also opens up opportunities when it's going up. If you invest $10 in a volatile investment, and that investment increases in value to $15 the next day, you've just made a 50 per cent return in a day. The trade-off is that something that can go up a lot in one day can just as easily go down a lot in one day.

In general, investments with higher volatility tend to be riskier than investments with lower volatility. That means they also tend to have potential for higher returns.

Volatility in your portfolio

Let's use an example to show how you can manage volatility.

Imagine a game at a carnival. Here's how it works: you give a mate some money, and they flip a coin. If it's heads, you get five times what you bet. If it's tails, you get nothing. This is a very volatile return — all or nothing.

Now let's say you have $5. You could bet it all at once. Heads, you get $25. Tails, you get nothing. Thanks for playing.

Here's another option. Rather than bet the $5 all at once, you make five bets in a row, for $1 each. If you win once, you've made your money back. If you win twice, you've doubled your investment. And given the odds of a coin toss are 50 per cent, that means it's pretty likely that you'll win at least once, and probably twice.

You might have figured out what we're getting at here — back to our old favourite, dollar-cost averaging. Dollar-cost averaging is when you behave like the person in the second situation, and invest small amounts, regularly, over a long time period. When things go down, your investments may lose value, but when they go up, any investments you made in the down period will rise in value. This helps to 'smooth out' volatility and gives you access to those bigger returns without taking as much risk.

One last thing to remember is that volatile investments and smoother, less volatile investments are not mutually exclusive. You can diversify by putting some money into something volatile, and put some other money into something less volatile. If you combine this with dollar-cost averaging, you can make that volatility even smoother — and give yourself a better chance of those good long-term returns.

As always, it's up to you how you handle volatility. Your investment portfolio could be 100 per cent volatile shares, 0 per cent volatile shares, or somewhere in between. What's more, you could invest $10 every week, $100 every 10 weeks, or another amount that works for you.

While volatility can be a rollercoaster, if you have a long time horizon, it may pay to stay on the ride. Holding on to a well-diversified set of investments for a long time gives you a better chance of turning your money into more money — and at the end of the day, that's what investing is all about.

Volatility is the aggressive investor's friend

You might have heard people talk about 'aggressive' investors — people who don't mind seeing their investment balance go up and down, probably because they aren't planning to sell up for a while.

They usually aren't counting on their investments for any income, either.

Conservative investors stay away from things that are risky or volatile but aggressive investors will jump in.

If your portfolio had $99 worth of Xero Limited (ASX:XRO) shares, and $1 worth of bond funds, that's a pretty aggressive portfolio — you're accepting and expecting a few ups and downs, for the chance of higher longer-term returns. If you had things switched the other way around, you'd have a conservative portfolio — you'd expect a pretty flat ride up the hill, but give up the chance of that ride being more of a mountain than a bump.

Why invest aggressively?

The golden rule of investing is that if you're willing to take more risk, you're also able to get a shot at better returns, so this is all probably sounding quite familiar.

The trade-off, as we mentioned with risk earlier in the book, is that there's a higher chance of going backwards as well as forwards.

People who invest aggressively take on a bit more risk and hopefully make more money.

If you're young, depending on your personal circumstances and future need for the money, your lengthy investing time horizon is a bit of a 'get out of jail free' card for the downside of taking more risk.

On the other hand, if you're in your late sixties and getting ready to retire, your circumstances might suggest leaning towards a more balanced or conservative approach, as you may want to start spending that money soon.

When is aggressive investing not the right approach?

Being young doesn't automatically make aggressive investing a natural fit for you.

It all comes down to your investing goal. If you're about to sell your shares to put a deposit on a house, then aggressive investing may not be for you — after all, the last thing you need is for your house deposit to shrink overnight from a market dip. We saw this quite a bit in 2020, when people who had become used to strong returns from their superannuation funds suddenly got a shock when they realised they were in the wrong fund for their needs.

Have a think about the way your investment's value today connects to your goals. If your goal is around the corner, then your investment losing value may affect your ability to reach that goal. But if your goal is years in the future, then a loss in value today or tomorrow isn't going to make a difference.

And remember — aggressive investing isn't an all-or-nothing deal. You can divide your portfolio up in any way you want, whether that's 100 per cent aggressive, 100 per cent conservative, or somewhere in between.

History's big crashes (and how long it took to recover from them)

1929: Great Depression

The worst sharemarket crash in history began in 1929, and sparked the Great Depression.

The decline began in September but really took hold in October of that year. On Black Tuesday, 29 October, the Dow Jones dropped by nearly 13 per cent.[30] The next day it dropped by another 12 per cent. By the middle of November, it had dropped in value by half but it didn't stop there — in 1932 it was 89 per cent below its peak. It returned to its pre-crash level in November 1954. At that point, the

---

30 'Stock Market Crash of 1929', Federal Reserve History (website), https://www.federalreservehistory.org/essays/stock-market-crash-of-1929

Dow Jones Industrial Average was sitting at about 382. In November 2021, it had hit 35,921.

The crash came after the 'Roaring Twenties', in which optimistic consumers racked up their purchases on credit and instalment plans and household debt rocketed. They also bought into the stock exchange with loans from banks or brokers.[31] Some people argue that the buying frenzy pushed prices beyond a sustainable level, but there was also a US interest rate hike and an agricultural recession. As with most other big collapses, once the problems started, panic spread among investors and things snowballed. While the crash would have been tough to deal with, the growth in the sharemarket since then proves how much time can wipe out even the biggest drops.

1987: Black Monday

Most of us have heard of the big sharemarket crash of the 1980s, sometimes referred to as 'Black Monday'.

It's become almost part of the New Zealand and Australian psyche, because it affected so many people in this part of the world. During the eighties, large numbers of people started buying shares and even set up share clubs to trade tips and strategise together. Then one day, it all came to an end.

There were a lot of factors that might have been to blame — falling oil prices and increasing US–Iran tensions, and maybe a US tax bill[32] that would have reduced the tax benefits associated

---

31 'What Caused the Stock Market Crash of 1929' HISTORY, (website),https://www.history.com/news/what-caused-the-stock-market-crash-of-1929
32 'Triggering the 1987 Stock Market Crash . . .', SEC Historical Society (website),https://www.sechistorical.org/collection/papers/1980/1989_0504_TriggeringAntitakeoverT.pdf

with financing mergers and leveraged buyouts. Increased use of computerised share-trading platforms was also pointed to as a factor because it made it easier for brokers to trade hard and fast.[33]

The crash affected much of the world — all 23 major world markets experienced a big drop that October — but we were more affected than most. It was particularly bad in New Zealand[34] because people were borrowing against their homes, farms and businesses to buy shares. Interest rates did not help — they were higher than 20 per cent. This left a lot of New Zealanders in a really tight spot.

But at the peak in September 1987, the NZX was at 3968.89. In November 2021, the NZX50 was sitting at more than 13,000. (That number is calculated based on the prices of shares in the companies that make up the index.) Are you seeing the theme here?

2000–02: The Dot-Com Bubble

Around the turn of the century, the internet was still new. There was a sense that it would be a goldmine — but no one was entirely sure exactly who was going to be able to make their fortunes from it.

There was a surge in interest in companies that had '.com' names and many attracted investment even if their business models were shaky.[35] Anything tech-y was seen as a good investment — even if it really wasn't. Investors piled into pretty much every internet start-up. But, as you have probably guessed, not every tech company turned into a goldmine. Some of their share prices were pretty hard to justify and eventually started to fall.

The tech-heavy Nasdaq index lost more than 75 per cent of

33 'The Crash', New Zealand Herald (website), https://www.nzherald.co.nz/indepth/business/1987-stock-market-crash/
34 Ibid.
35 'Who Drove and Burst the Tech Bubble?', https://www.jstor.org/stable/29789815

its value between March 2000 and October 2002,[36] and companies like Pets.com and Toys.com went out of business completely. Pets.com is a good example of the heat in the market at that time. It was an online platform for customers to order pet supplies, and raised US$82.5 million in an IPO in February 2000,[37] where its shares started trading at US$11 each. But the company's revenue didn't start rolling in as planned. When Pets.com was to be liquidated in November of that year,[38] its shares were changing hands for about $0.20.[39] At the time, media said the retailer (and others that suffered a similar fate) weren't offering customers a compelling reason to shop online.[40] Maybe it was just ahead of its time.

Some 'tech' shares have been extremely solid performers since then. In 2001, Apple Inc. (NASDAQ:AAPL) shares were changing hands for as low as US$0.30. Twenty years later, they were worth almost US$150 each.

2007–08: The GFC

Subprime mortgages get the blame for sparking the Global Financial Crisis, or GFC.[41] Lenders were giving money to American borrowers who weren't able to meet the loan repayments. Investors then

---

36 'Dotcom Bubble', CFI (website), https://corporatefinanceinstitute. com/resources/knowledge/trading-investing/dotcom-bubble/
37 'Pets.com raises $82.5 million in IPO', CNET (website), https:// www.cnet.com/news/pets-com-raises-82-5-million-in-ipo/
38 'Pets.com at its tail end', CNN Money (website), https://money.cnn. com/2000/11/07/technology/pets/
39 'Why did Pets.com Crash So Drastically', Investopedia (website), https://www.investopedia.com/ask/answers/08/dotcom-pets-dot-com.asp
40 'The Failure of Pets.com', (web page), http://www.uky. edu/~dsianita/695ec/failure.html
41 'Revisiting Subprime Pricing Irrationality During the Global Financial Crisis', https://elischolar.library.yale.edu/cgi/viewcontent. cgi?article=1185&context=Journal-of-financial-crises

bought mortgage-backed securities and other investment vehicles that were based on 'subprime' loans. When the inevitable happened and some of those borrowers started to default on their loans, things got pretty shaky quickly.

Property prices also fell significantly in many parts of the United States and the mortgage-backed securities lost value, taking the stock market down with them as concerns grew about the extent to which global banks were exposed. Some big companies that had invested a lot of money in real estate securities completely failed, most memorably Lehman Brothers Holdings Inc. Its shock bankruptcy caused a lot of investors to panic.

In New Zealand and Australia, problems in the core banking system during the crisis were relatively mild.[42] None of our major banks fell over, although a lot of retirees were burned by the failure of a number of finance companies whose investment offerings were riskier than many of their investors realised.[43]

The Reserve Bank of New Zealand said the stability of the main banks through the credit crunch was a reflection of our more 'vanilla-flavoured' banking sector and relatively sound bank capital structures. There was little exposure to complex instruments and opaque interconnections in our markets — our banks weren't packaging up shaky mortgages and selling them on.

But the crisis caused a collapse in confidence, for both businesses and consumers. Unemployment increased significantly. From the peak to its lowest point, investors in the NZX50 lost 44 per

---

42 'Learnings from the Global Financial Crisis', RBNZ (website),https://www.rbnz.govt.nz/research-and-publications/speeches/2012/speech2012-08-09
43 'Finance company collapses, 2006-2012 (New Zealand)', Wikipedia (website),https://en.wikipedia.org/wiki/Finance_company_collapses,_2006–2012_(New_Zealand)

cent of their investment value but, importantly, it only took about two years for markets to recover.

March 2020: The Covid crash

This crash is a bit of a strange one because, while the drop was big and painful, it was short-lived and was followed by a big bounce. It dramatically highlights how important it is to stick with a fall.

As Covid-19 spread around the world and the impact of the pandemic became more apparent, investors worried about what it would mean for business fortunes. Prices fell fast.

The New Zealand sharemarket suffered its biggest one-day fall since 1987[44] and the S&P 500 took just 22 days to fall 30 per cent — its fastest drop ever.[45]

But markets also bounced back quickly — the S&P 500 was back to pre-pandemic levels about six months later. 'Money printing' by central governments around the world and a big fall in interest rates encouraged the flow of money into investment markets, which enabled prices to recover.

People started talking about not only FOMO (Fear of Missing Out) driving the sharemarket recovery, but also TINA (There Is No Alternative). Investors had nowhere else to put their money, which helped to drive share prices up, even if the outlook remained worrying.

The ASX dropped to a low of 4853 but by August the following year it was back at levels that preceded its pre-drop peak of 7096.

44 'NZ stock market suffers biggest session drop since 1987 crash', RNZ (website), https://www.rnz.co.nz/news/business/412382/nz-stock-market-suffers-biggest-session-drop-since-1987-crash
45 'This was the fastest 30% sell-off ever . . .', CNBC (website), https://www.cnbc.com/2020/03/23/this-was-the-fastest-30percent-stock-market-decline-ever.html

Fund manager advice

Mike Taylor, CEO and Founder of PIE Funds investment manager says, 'Volatile markets are a big part of investing. There are a great couple of quotes from investment guru's Warren Buffet and his 98-year-old offsider Charlie Munger, who together have the best track record of any investor, ever. Warren says, "Be greedy when others are fearful, and fearful when they are greedy," and Charlie says, "The wise ones bet heavily when they have the odds. The rest of the time they don't."

'I learnt these lessons early on in my career and they have helped me greatly when things get a little crazy out there. They are as valuable today as when they first said them, and it doesn't matter what you are investing in, or how experienced you are, knowing when to buy and when to sell, are just as important as what to buy. Great companies don't always make great investments if you get your timing wrong.'

Investor story: Riding out a downturn

Kelvin remembers looking at ways he could be boosting his saving efforts, and being underwhelmed at what was on offer from term deposits.

'Interest rates were quite low,' he says, 'so I was looking at other investment options. I remember my friends talking about Sharesies so I did a bit of research on that. Then I saw that stock markets generally return a lot better, especially if you're looking at a longer period of time. I decided to invest in exchange-traded funds (ETFs). Friends said really good things about Sharesies so I made an account and that was the start of it.'

Most of his portfolio is in ETFs but he also invests directly in shares in companies that he knows well 'or when I really believe in the product'.

Kelvin says he takes almost a 'lazy' approach these days, with an auto-invest global order set up to diversify his investments each month, without him having to do very much or make too many decisions.

'It's a good way of putting money there and knowing it's going to diversify itself. The returns have been pretty good, it's worked out well and I'm pleased with how easy the whole thing is. It's returning a lot better than term deposits.'

He says he'll keep putting money aside in Sharesies and build up as much as he can. His long-term plan is to use the money to buy a house or start a business.

'It's nice knowing the money is there and it's growing at a good rate, so whatever I choose in the future I'll have it there.'

He says he puts aside as much as he can each month when he is paid, depending on what expenses he knows are coming up.

Kelvin says that when he first started investing, he was worried about the prospect of markets falling. That wasn't helped by the fact that he first tested the waters just before the pandemic spooked markets.

'I remember seeing in early 2020 that the markets all crashed in March because of Covid. I was really worried that I was going to lose all this money.'

Now, with a bit more time in the market and some greater understanding of what to expect, he is less concerned.

'I've learnt now to look at shares as a long-term investment. Over the long term the dips even themselves out — it's about riding the trend rather than looking at the dips.'

Investing has also meant some learning more about the financial market in general, he said. He now knows much more about markets and listens to podcasts about how the economy works, as well as researching sharemarkets.

Kelvin says Sharesies is a good option for other new investors, too, and might be easier than they think.

'It's been quite interesting. I'd recommend starting small if you're unsure and going from there. It is really easy. There's a perception that investing in shares is a daunting task, that you have to go through a broker and need contracts, but it's actually really easy. It's just an account on a website and start investing from there.'

What now?

- Remind yourself why you are investing, and why you've chosen the investments you are in.
- Remember what's happened in the past — markets do wobble (and crash) but they usually come back stronger.
- Understand what sort of volatility your portfolio is exposed to and what that might feel like.
- Write 'future you' a note about why you're investing and refer back to it, so that you have a strategy to draw on when prices are falling.
- Get help if you need it, from a licensed financial advisor.

9.

The rest of your financial life

By now, you should have a pretty solid idea of how to go about investing in shares, and rolling with whatever the investment world throws your way.

But the investing side of your financial life is just one piece of the puzzle. If you really want to grow your wealth, you'll need to have the rest of your finances in order, too.

Here are some things to think about. Also worth noting, the following is intended as general advice only — everyone's situation is unique. You'll need to consider your personal circumstances before making any investment decisions, as well as the benefits and risks of investing. And know you can always seek independent financial advice if you need it.

Your budget

People often think of a 'budget' as something restrictive that is only useful to people who don't have much money coming in each week.

While it's true that budgeting is essential if you're on a tight income, it is helpful for people right across the wealth spectrum.

To really improve your financial situation, you need to have a clear view of how much money you earn, and how much money you spend. In other words: a budget.

Having a budget gives you control. If you know where your money is going each month, it's a lot easier to make adjustments to help you reach your financial goals.

It's also a great opportunity to allocate some of your money into things that you enjoy and that make you feel good. This is a chance to double-check you're consciously spending on the things you love, not just frittering your money away on expenses that don't give you any return (financial, emotional, or otherwise).

Even if you don't end up making any changes, it's still worth going through the budgeting process from time to time to remind yourself where your money is going.

There's nothing inherently wrong in any kind of spending — even going out for the infamous avocado on toast — as long as you have made the conscious decision to allow for that in your budget, and you're getting something out of it.

It's easy to think of a budget as a real fun sponge, where you're meticulously tracking every single cent you spend, trying to spend as little as humanly possible and telling your friends you'll see them in 2043 when you've saved the amount of money you require. In fact, a good budget should take into account the money you need to spend on the things you enjoy right now.

Step 1: How much are you earning and spending?

First off, you want to see how much you're earning, and how much you're spending. The best place to find this out is through your online banking. Download three months of online banking transactions — three months is a good number because it should include most of those infrequent but costly expenses like dental bills and car repairs.

Now, it's time to get adding. You want to find out how much you spend and how much you earn.

The 'how much you earn' bit is likely to be straightforward, unless you're getting your income from your own business, or you're a contractor or temp worker with fluctuating income. Work out exactly what you get in the hand (after tax) each pay period, or what your average income is per week over the three months.

Then, count up your spending.

You can do this by putting your transactions in a spreadsheet, using a personal finance app, adding it all up on your calculator, or your banking app may have a feature that helps with this. Your internet banking history is your friend. Try to put together a breakdown of what you've spent over the past three months.

Then, divide your total spending by the number of pay periods in the three months.

If you're paid once a week, you'll divide your total by 12. If you get paid fortnightly, you'll divide by six. And if you're paid once a month — you guessed it — divide by three.

That will give you an amount coming in each period, and an amount going out.

Now you have a really clear view of how much you spend against how much you earn. Ideally, you'll have a surplus. If you're in deficit, spending more than you earn, your budget might need a bit of surgery.

Step 2: Get categorising

After you've figured out how much you make and how much you

spend, you can get into the details by dividing your spending into categories.

Your rent or mortgage payments will probably be your biggest category, so start with that one. Then work your way down. Keep your categories broad to make the process easier. You could track your takeaway coffee, lunches, meals out with friends and drinks at bars, all in the same category of 'meals out'. That's a lot easier than painstakingly dividing everything into separate categories. Same goes for things like power, internet and phone bills. Just wrap these all into one category called 'utilities'.

Finally, don't feel like you need to account for every single dollar you spend. Start with the big categories first, and work your way down. If you work through a few categories, and you've accounted for 90 per cent of your spending, don't worry about that last 10 per cent. Just call it all 'other'.

Step 3: Drill down further and choose some priorities

Now that everything is divided into broad categories, you can go into more detail where you need to. For example, if the 'meals out' category is sucking up a lot of your money, you could categorise that spending further to find out why. Are you spending loads on takeaway coffee? Or are you going out to bars four times a week?

Next, it's time to make some decisions. What spending truly makes you happy? Is it the money you spent with friends, the donation to charity, your investments? And on the other side, what could you cut out? Is there spending in your transaction history on things that you don't even remember buying? If you can make these decisions about the things that are eating up the biggest portion of your budget, you'll be focusing on the areas that will make the biggest impact.

Step 4: Build your budget

Now it's time to build your budget. There are all kinds of ways you can do this, but here are a few examples:

- You can be very specific and set a certain amount to spend on each category. This is a pretty effective way of getting your spending on track but you need to have a certain type of personality to stick with something regimented for a decent length of time.
- You can have a 50/30/20 budget: 50 per cent of your money goes on your needs (like rent and groceries), 30 per cent on wants (like going to the movies, or travelling), 20 per cent on savings (or investments).
- You can divide your disposable income (money remaining after key expenses and Superannuation is covered) into three: spend a third of your income, invest a third of your income, and give a third of your income to charities or people in your life you can support.
- You can have an 80/20 budget: invest 20 per cent of your income, then the rest is yours to do whatever you want with. This is a strategy for people who don't want to think about it too much.
- You can set a daily budget. These budgets are pretty simple, but you still need to find out where your money's going before you start using one. That way, if you do an 80/20 budget (for example), you know where you need to make cuts to free up 20 per cent of your income for investing.

The choice is yours.

Step 5: Track and check in

Once you've created your budget, be sure to check back in now and again. This doesn't need to be an arduous process. You just need to take a look at your spending, and compare it to your budget. Are you sticking to the budget you set for yourself? Or are you missing it? What's causing the misses? If you need to make changes, what would those changes look like?

When you're doing this, remember that if something isn't working for you, you can always change it. There's no point in persisting with a budget that isn't doing what it's meant to. Over the course of a few months, experiment with a few different budgeting approaches until you find something that works. After all, it's your money, so manage it your way.

Your budget will not be set in stone. As your circumstances, commitments and income change, so too will the way you manage your money.

Debt: not always a dirty word

For lots of people, debt is just another four-letter word. It's something they want to avoid at all costs.

But in the modern world, that's pretty hard to do. Most of us have a few credit cards, maybe a hire purchase, or a few things we've bought using buy now, pay later services.

While some debt can create bad financial situations, debt isn't always bad. In some cases, it can be a great tool to improve your life. Think of your student loan, or the mortgage you use to buy your house. If you choose the right course of study, and invest wisely in a property, these can be tools to much greater wealth in the long term. But a loan to buy a pricey piece of jewellery that depreciates the minute you put it on isn't adding to your financial health at all.

Consider your car (if you have one). Your car is probably very useful for getting around, doing your shopping, and so on. But imagine if you never wore a seatbelt, always looked at your phone while driving and never drove slower than 140 kph. Then your car would be much less useful and much more dangerous. Debt is the same. Used correctly, debt can be useful. And used dangerously, debt can be something out of *Fast & Furious*.

Debt is either secured or unsecured. A secured debt is when someone lends you money, but gets the right to take something from you if you don't pay it back.

A car loan is a good example. If you borrow money to buy a car, but don't make your debt repayments, the company you borrowed the money from will take the car and sell it to recover the amount they lent you. In that scenario, the lender only loses the difference between what it is owed and what it can sell the car for.

If you're wondering why a borrower would sign up for a deal like that, the answer is in the interest rate. If a lender knows you have something of value, and it also knows it has the right to sell it, then that is less risky for the lender. If the lender is taking on less risk, it can charge you less interest.

If you buy a car with an unsecured loan, like a credit card, then stop making your repayments, the credit card company needs to try and get that money off you. It won't necessarily know that you have a car, and the process to take it from you and sell it is going to be harder than it would be if the debt was secured, so the lender may well lose the entire loan.

How does it protect themselves? It charges a higher interest rate.

That's the trade-off to think about when you're looking at debt. If an interest rate is low, it will be because the lender thinks there is less risk — and if the interest rate is high, it thinks it is taking lots of risk.

Do a stocktake of your debt — do you have debt that is costing you a lot of money? Getting rid of expensive (high-interest) debt is a priority. Here are a few strategies to try:

Snowball

The snowball method involves focusing on paying off your smallest debt first, then moving on to the next smallest, and so on. This strategy is really helpful for people who need lots of wins to keep them motivated. You can celebrate every time you get rid of one of your debts.

Avalanche

With this method, you rank all your debts according to the interest rate you're being charged, and attack the highest-interest rate loan first. Put any extra money you can into that loan and simply make the minimum payments on the others. Pay it off and then move to the next. This is the cheapest way to pay off debt because you're getting rid of the most expensive loans first. This is generally what budgeting advisors will tell you to do.

Blizzard

This is a mixture of both — a snowball to get you motivated, then an avalanche for the rest of your balances.

Don't make the minimum payment for long

Be very careful about making the minimum payment on any of your debts. Sometimes, for example with hire-purchase debts, the minimum payment isn't enough to clear the debt before the end of an interest-free period. With credit cards, minimum payments can be very bad news.

Credit card companies will often ask you to pay a minimum amount each month such as 3 per cent or 5 per cent of the amount you owe. But if you owe $5000 and only pay it off at 4 or 5 per cent a month with an interest rate of 18.5 per cent, you'll end up paying almost $2000 extra in interest charges.

Give yourself a regular financial check-up

While you're getting your financial life in order, it's worth scheduling a regular check-up to keep yourself on track. Set a reminder in your phone or a calendar notification to pop up and tell you when it's time to look at things in a bit more depth again.

One study estimated that 80 per cent of New Year's resolutions are abandoned by February. People usually slip up and don't stick to their big goals and aspirations; it's actually uncommon for people to not go off track.

So be kind to yourself. Don't worry if you don't always stick to your budget, or put as much as you were hoping into your investments or savings.

But you also need to be honest with yourself. Get out those bank accounts and investment portfolios and run through them every few months. Once you know how on-track (or off-track) you are, you can start making a plan — but you need to know what you're dealing with first. Putting your head in the sand is not a sound financial strategy.

Do you need to adjust your goal?

If you're nowhere close to hitting your investment goals, you can always adjust them. They are your goals, after all. Consider what's going wrong. Maybe your goal was too ambitious, or your situation has changed and you have less money to invest than you thought you would have. Or maybe your goal is not the same as it was three months ago.

Either way, the key is to be realistic about what you can do. It's much better to choose an affordable amount to put aside each week or month, that you can sustain over time, than to choose an overly ambitious amount, which you abandon when it gets too hard. In other words, it's better to invest something than to invest nothing at all.

If your goal has changed, or it's too hard to reach it, go ahead and change it. Not everyone gets their budgets right the first time and it may be that you need to allow for a bit more slack in yours than you expected.

This doesn't necessarily have to mean changing the investment amount you're aiming for, either. You can adjust your timeframe as well as adjusting the total amount you want to invest. If you decide you want to achieve your goal in 10 years instead of seven years, you can put aside less each week — or vice versa if you want to achieve your goal faster.

On top of this, remember that your goal can go both ways. If you need to reduce it by a little bit for now, that doesn't mean it needs to stay there forever. Once you drop your regular payment to a sustainable level, you could try to gradually increase it. Maybe you invest $10 this week, and $11 next week, then $12, and so on. Little by little, you'll build an investing habit and adjust your spending habits around it.

Can you split your goal into chunks?

One of the pitfalls of long-term investing or saving is that it can feel like a real slog, especially in the early days. Let's say you want to invest $10,000 over five years. That's equivalent to investing about $40 a week.

If you diligently invest $40 a week for three months, you would have invested $480 in your investment account — plus or minus any returns. It's a start, but it's not $10,000. A lot of people might get demoralised at this point and give up. An investment of $480 feels a lot closer to zero than $10,000.

You can short-circuit these unhelpful thought patterns by breaking your goal into chunks.

Let's look at that $10,000 in five years another way. It's actually $2000 a year, for five years. So rather than a big goal of $10,000, you are aiming for a much more reasonable goal of $2000. Next year, your goal will be another $2000 — and so on for three more years after that.

We know that this is exactly the same thing as saving up $10,000. But humans aren't rational. If we recognise this fact, and change our behaviour around it, we can essentially 'trick' ourselves into achieving our goals.

Getting those returns

There's another advantage to this approach: it makes your investment account look even better. Remember, you're investing, not saving — so your investments should generally grow over time.

For example, let's say you put aside $2000 at the start of your first year. The market goes up and down, but on average, you might get a 5 per cent return for that particular year. If you manage that, your balance at the end of the year would be around $2100. If you put away another $2000 at the start of the next year, and then earn another 5 per cent return, your balance would be at $4305 — you've gone above and beyond your goal. Over time, this all really adds up.

Don't just run this check-up once — check back again in a few months, then check back again a few months after that. You'll be surprised at how quickly your income, personal situation, risk tolerance and goals will change. Regularly checking in is the best way to keep investing the amount you need to get the things you want.

Is investing in shares a substitute for buying a house?

If you're reading this book, you're obviously interested in investing in shares. But for many people, home ownership is still a major life goal.

While it's totally possible to build large amounts of wealth by investing in shares, there are still reasons why it might not take the place of property purchases in your financial strategy.

While investing in a house does give you somewhere to live, property isn't necessarily the best (or only) investment you can make. With this in mind, we thought we'd work through some of the benefits of investing in a home and investing in shares.

Tick for housing: putting debt to work

We've already covered the difference between types of debt. Mortgages can often be very useful debt, for a couple of reasons:

- Mortgages are basically a guaranteed savings plan. You have to make regular payments towards your home loan, or the bank will take your house off you. A portion of those payments helps to pay off your loan — resulting in you owning more and more of your house over time. If you pay off some of your home loan that has a 5 per cent interest rate, that gives you roughly the same effect as putting money into a savings account that pays 5 per cent (after tax). As a risk-free return, that's pretty good.

- It's a lot easier to be disciplined about paying your mortgage than it is to stay disciplined about saving money every week. The bank's not going to let you miss a payment just because you have other things you might want to do with your money. Buying a house more or less forces you into saving money by investing in your property instead of paying rent.

- A mortgage gives you leverage. When you put down a deposit to buy a house, you are investing just a portion of the house's total value, and having the bank take care of the rest (in exchange for interest). If the house grows in value at a faster rate than your interest rate, then you'll automatically be getting some pretty solid gains. It is much harder to come by leverage if you're investing in shares in New Zealand (particularly as finding lending for share investments is often expensive).

Tick for housing: all about control

When you own a house, you have more control over its value. When you buy shares in a company (or group of companies), there's not a lot you can do to change their value. If the companies do well, you'll get a nice return, and if they don't do very well, you won't — it's not so easy to go into the boardroom and force the bosses to run the company the way you want it to be run.

With housing, you have a lot more control. You can save some money and improve your home — for example, splash a lick of paint on the walls, or add another whole bedroom. If you wanted to, you might even be able to knock your house down and build two houses in its place.

Tick for shares: financial flexibility

Let's take a closer look at the control you have over your house. While it's true that you can increase your home's value by investing in improvements, it's also true that improvements are expensive. You'd have a hard time finding a way to improve a house for $5 a week.

Shares, on the other hand, have a lot more flexibility. You can invest much smaller amounts in shares, and you don't need to save a deposit.

Shares also come with less hassle. Even if you had thousands of dollars to upgrade your home, investing in your home would involve hiring tradespeople, getting materials delivered, and living in a construction site for a while. With shares, there's far less effort involved: you just choose to buy some shares, and a couple of days later, they're yours.

This flexibility also works for selling. You can't really sell a part of your house. The closest you could get is renting out a bedroom, which comes with its own set of annoyances. With shares, it's just as easy to sell some of them as it is to sell all of them. With housing, it's usually an all-or-nothing deal.

Tick for shares: lifestyle flexibility

One of the great things about shares is that they follow you wherever you go. They don't need any maintenance or management either — they just sit there, regardless of what you do or where you live.

This can be a major benefit, depending on your lifestyle. For example, one of the best ways to increase your salary is to change jobs. Some people make the most of this by hopping jobs every couple of years, and moving cities to do so. If your lifestyle looks like this, then shares can be a much easier investment than a house. If you get a great job offer in a different city, you can just pack up and leave. You don't need to rent out your shares, or get someone to look after them.

This flexibility is particularly useful when you compare it to the first few years of home ownership, when mortgage payments and other costs (like rates and insurance) will probably be higher than what you could get renting your house out.

If you don't want to own a home, shares can be a great way to put your money to work, without having too much of an impact on your lifestyle.

Tick for both: diversification

However, it's not an all-or-nothing deal. If you want to buy a house, and are able to do so, there's no reason that property needs to be your only investment. We're all about diversification, and housing is no exception.

If you own a home, you can protect yourself from the ups and downs of property investment by also investing in shares. Here are some ways that this approach could help you:

- By investing some of your wealth in shares, you can protect yourself from losing all your wealth if your specific house decreases in value. For example, your roof falling in has a big impact on the value of your house, but no effect on the value of your share investments.
- You can protect yourself from regional economic problems by investing in overseas shares. For example, if you own a

house in NZ, you could invest in the Smartshares US 500
ETF (NZX:USF). That way, if something happens to the
NZ economy and your home loses value, you have some of
your wealth invested in the American economy.

It's all about staying diverse. This approach opens you up to more
opportunities, and it can also protect you from some of the down-
sides of investment. In other words? You can have it all, if you want.

What's the answer?

You've probably realised by now that there's no hard-and-fast answer
to this question. Rather, it's about your personal circumstances and
goals. Investing in property may not be for everyone, and investing
in shares may not be for everyone. The key is to take a hard look at
what you want and when you want it, then make your investment
decisions based on what works best for you.

If you decide that investing in property is something you really
want to do, investing in shares can be an excellent way to build your
deposit to get there.

Talking with the kids

Kids are so rich with the world's most valuable asset, time. For
lots of people, a really important financial goal is to pass on their
knowledge and financial skills to the kids in their lives, making sure
they're set up for the future.

This is a great goal, but it can sometimes feel like it's easier
said than done.

There are some general rules to live by if you want to help kids
to become financially savvy and ready to take on the money world.

Talk about money

Being super secretive or feeling awkward about money conversations is a sure-fire way to make your kids think that money is a mystery that they'll never get the hang of.

Try to make discussions about money — your spending, investing, saving and debt — as normal in your household as conversations about what you're going to have for dinner.

Even if it feels a bit awkward at first, push yourself to make money just another topic you talk about.

Talk about your work and what you're paid and how you grow your money for the future. Get the kids to help you work out which are the better deals when you do your supermarket shopping. If you're tossing up between two purchases and can't afford to buy both, talk about how you're making that decision. Talk to kids about how you make decisions about which companies to invest in.

In short, be open about your investing journey with your kids, sharing your financial mistakes as well as your successes.

Lead by example

Show the kids some practical examples of how you're using your money knowledge.

If you're saving up for something, talk about how that works and how you're progressing towards the goal. Talk about your investments and the strategies you're following — as well as how you'll know when you get there.

If things aren't going so well, explain what's happened and how you plan to get back on track. If you're invested in a company that's having a bad month, point that out and let kids know why you still think it's a worthwhile investment.

Give them chances to practise

Let the kids have a go at managing their money while it's still low-stakes. Give them an allowance (whether that's for chores or a set amount is up for debate but entirely up to you) and then ask them to set themselves a budget. Some could be for spending, some for saving, some for investing — you might also suggest they give some to charity.

Let them experiment with their money and work out how to balance their own budgets — and try to resist the temptation to bail them out when they run out of money. At least, don't do it too often!

Some people choose to buy a few shares for their kids (or to start investing more seriously) so that the kids can understand how markets work and watch their investments, with the benefit of a very long time horizon, which allows them to take on a bit of extra risk.

We know of so many people who are supporting kids to start to understand investing. That might be parents who chat about Sharesies at the dinner table, talking about how their portfolios are going and why they may have gone up or down depending on the events of that day. Or grandparents who, any time they are tempted to buy clothes or toys for their grandchildren, put that money instead into a grandchild's Sharesies account for their future. Maybe aunties and uncles who put money into kids' Sharesies accounts for their birthdays and other special events in their lives.

Giving an investment as a gift is a gift that keeps on giving.

Investor story: Thanks to Mum

Michelle has her mother to thank for her investment journey. She had always had her money in savings accounts, but noticed the interest rate she could get was dropping. Once tax was deducted, Michelle felt like she was going backwards. A move to term deposits didn't help much, because those interest rates just kept falling.

'Mum said, "Why don't you try investing in an investment portfolio?" she recalls.

Michelle, who is a student, started sending some money to an investment advisory firm that invested it for her. But she didn't enjoy the lack of control over where her money was invested. 'Mum suggested I take a look at Sharesies.'

Michelle liked the idea of being able to choose where her money went. 'I tried it out and loved it.'

She started with a similar approach to that she had taken with the investment advisors, putting a chunk of money into a fund and then leaving it.

'Then I realised the benefit of being able to buy companies and different things is that I can diversify,' she says. 'I set up an automatic payment for funds — I have 20 different funds I buy once a week. At the same time I have 25 companies I buy once a week as well, on the same day, the same amount every week. Companies don't have an automatic payment option yet so I do it manually. I set an alarm and every Monday after the market opens I go through and buy $5 of each company's shares.'

Returns have been good so far; after three years Michelle had made a 27 per cent return. 'When I reached 10 per cent I remembered how I used to struggle for 3.7 per cent on a term deposit and I had no idea what was happening with the money. It's been growing over time — the percentage and the value of the portfolio. Every time I reach a milestone like 10 per cent, 15 per cent, 20 per cent I think wow!'

Michelle says she wasn't initially sold on the idea of automatic investments but came around to it.

'I didn't think I would want to set up automatic payments because I wanted to watch the market and buy at the right time, but I realised trying to time the market is a waste of time unless you're sitting in front of a computer 24/7. If you have a normal job outside investing you can't afford to do that.'

Michelle has been through two market drops so far. The first was with the investment advisors, when her initial $1000 investment dropped quickly to $600.

'It was a month after I invested. I cried my eyes out, saying to Mum, 'What have I done? This is awful.' Then in the next four to six months my investment recovered back to that $1000 and then went into positive. The initial experience showed me the worst thing straight away and everything else was good.'

When the market dropped in 2020, she was ready. 'This time because I knew it was going to recover I had a completely different attitude. My initial response was to buy more shares because everything is on sale and it's just going to go up.

'I remember I was in a tutorial and the tutor gave us a 10-minute break and I said, "I have to go and buy shares." People were saying, "Didn't the market just drop, isn't now a really bad time for investors?" But I said, "No, it's the opposite, it's great." They all thought I was crazy but that worked out really well for me.'

Michelle says she's only sold two or three investments in the past three years because they were not performing, and she has not withdrawn any money from her Sharesies account at all.

She no longer has a separate savings account and puts all the money beyond what she needs for her daily transactions into her Sharesies account. 'It's essentially my other bank account. It's going to make me money there even if it's there for a month. In a bank account it's not making me money.'

Michelle would have got started earlier if she'd realised she didn't need a lot of money to get underway. 'Because I've been a student throughout my investing journey, I thought I couldn't invest if I didn't have a lot of money. I've never had a regular proper income and I thought that I wasn't good enough to invest because I'm not as well off as other people.

'But even when I was investing $20 a week it was still worth it, it accumulated and it helped to get me used to it. I wouldn't have been comfortable to start off investing $500 a week.'

What now?

- If you don't already have a budget, have a go at making one. This will help put you in control of your money.
- Check out your debt — is any of it uncomfortable? If so, work out the best strategy to blast it.
- Think about your financial life as a whole — how do your share investments fit in with your other goals? Are you on track more broadly?
- Schedule regular financial check-ups to keep yourself in check. Get an accountability buddy if you need one. You could also join social media groups where people chat about personal finance and investing.

10.

The end (and the beginning)

By now, you should have a pretty good idea of how to craft an effective investment strategy to create an awesome future for yourself, your family — and the wider world. You have your head around the basics of doing your due diligence, riding out market wobbles and cashing in on compounding interest.

But while we're coming to the end of this book, we're also at a really exciting beginning — the start of the rest of your investment journey.

We want to leave you with three key messages to help guide you through the rest of your investing life, whether you invest in shares or other assets in the future.

And remember — your investment strategy and pathway isn't fixed. The route you embark on now, or the plan that feels right for you in this moment, doesn't have to be the same one you're treading in five years' time, let alone ten.

We hope we've given you all the tools and resources you need to change your plan as you go along, achieving greater and greater success.

Rule #1 for building your financial future

Believe in yourself

If this sounds a bit like something you'd read on an inspirational poster with a photo of a lion cub . . . bear with us.

Self-belief is very important when it comes to investing — you could say it's the secret ingredient that sets the success stories apart from the not-quite-theres.

It's something that a lot of us lack, because we assume we aren't good at investing. We think that because we haven't been let into some sort of top-secret money club, investing is not for us. We worry that because our parents didn't have anything to do with investing, or worse had been burned by it, that we don't have a chance. Good news! That's totally wrong.

No matter who you are and how much money you have, you can start investing and you can do really well. You don't need a flash car and a fat bank account to become a serious investor. You don't even need a sharebroker, if you're keen to do it yourself.

Even if you only have $5 a week to put away, if you do that over a long period of time, you'll end up with a decent amount of money. Time can be as important an asset in investing as the initial cash you have at your disposal. That's great news for people who are young and not super rich but have big dreams.

Give investing a go. Start small and start wherever you are. Do what you are comfortable with and grow from there. If you are only happy to invest in names you know well for now, that's fine. Get in there and learn how the market works. The most important thing is to just start and then keep going, putting one investment foot in front of the other.

You will learn from the experience every day and get better all the time. Once you honestly believe that you can be an investor, and that the investment world is accessible to you, you'll be surprised at what potential lies ahead. It's just about changing your beliefs and backing yourself. Chat to yourself as if you were your own best friend — what would you tell that person to get them motivated?

Think about what happens when you take out a gym membership — you usually believe that you'll be committed to making exercise a part of your life, and jump in all motivated by success. However, it's only by showing up regularly and slogging out the workouts that you make those fitness goals happen (or not). Investing is kind of the opposite — the 'pain point' is when you make the leap into investing and overcome your fears to get started. From there you can automate your commitment and make your investments happen (or your money go to the gym, if you like that metaphor) without even having to think about it. That is something that's pretty hard to do with workouts. The regular part of investing should become easy once you take that first step to get going.

You don't have to get all your investment decisions 100 per cent right. While it's easy to be a bit of a perfectionist and want to get everything right, that can become a big roadblock. Some people hang back from starting because they become paralysed by the need to make the correct decision all the time. They worry they're getting in at a point where prices are high, or when something bad is about to hit the sharemarket. But what looks like a wrong move today could turn out to be a right one in the long term. There are still people who are on the sidelines of the property market who said they were waiting for the bubble to burst 15 years ago.

Letting go of the need to be right all the time can be an important part of getting started. You won't be perfect, you won't be spot on all the time, but the more time you have in the market, the more chance you have of getting it right in the long term. Just be conscious of the natural impulses that might get in your way — things like the loss aversion and herd mentality that we talked about earlier are sometimes a threat to investor returns. Be mindful of them and keep referring back to your strategy and your own plan. Stay the course!

Rule #2 for building your financial future

Talk about it

Start chatting with your friends and family about investing opportunities, so you can start taking others along with you on your investing journey. You don't need to see money as a solo endeavour, because by definition share investing is an opportunity to come together in something. Share ownership means the ownership of a company is spread around a lot of people. It's a joint effort, and it's great to include the people in your world in your experiences.

Making investing and your financial life a part of your everyday conversations helps to break down any stigma that remains among the people you care about. Show them how easy and straightforward it can be to take steps for a better financial future, and to make improvements in the world.

You might be instrumental in helping someone make a major change for a better future.

Rule #3 for building your financial future

The way money flows changes the world

You might think you're just one person with a small amount of money to invest — what difference could you really make? Think about it this way instead — if everyone invests a small amount, it can make a huge change. If you're excited for the future and feel motivated to do something about it, investing is a way to create the future you want to live in. Money can be the tool that allows you to live the life you want to lead, in the world you want to live in.

There is real change going on through shareholder advocacy and investors getting involved with businesses they care about. More and more retail investors are getting on board, and this power in numbers is going to be a major force in the market.

Investing can be a step towards not just empowering yourself but empowering the community. More people are investing and putting their money into businesses, knowing their money is working in the background to create the world they want to see. One of the biggest impacts we can have is through what our money does on its journey towards our financial wealth. The more people involved, the more say we can all have on what the businesses we own do in the future.

Businesses are made up of people. The ownership of that company lies with its shareholders. Investment is about taking your share in the world and standing up for your right to be heard.

The financial world is changing

We can see a future soon where people will be as comfortable with the idea of investing in shares as they are with opening a savings account at the bank.

We want to get to the point where anyone can feel like they can be an investor and know how to go about it. There's already growing awareness through things like superannuation savings (KiwiSaver in New Zealand) because the amounts that most people have set aside in this scheme are becoming significant enough that they demand attention. People who thought they weren't investors are looking at their KiwiSaver balances and realising that they actually are.

Another factor driving change is that fewer people are buying their own homes. As more people decide that buying their own property is out of reach, they may find that putting money into share-based investments is a good alternative. It will not be long before their share portfolios are their most significant investment and source of wealth.

We can see a world where people think of investing in the same way as going to work each day. You go to work for a set number of hours in a day and exchange that time for money, contributing to a business or organisation to help it grow. In the same way that you show up for work every day, investors might start to think of their money going off to work every day, too, working for the growth of other companies and being rewarded for that.

The younger generation have different opportunities to grow their wealth now. Without reigniting a generational battle, we can say that the opportunities aren't necessarily better or bigger, but they are different to what our parents faced when they were starting out.

Technology is enabling new directions and investing opportunities and the financial world is becoming more and more democratised.

Young people are starting to see time as more of a resource than their parents did. The older generations had a focus on a job for life, and thought that a steady job was a measure of success. Now, we're more likely to see people holding portfolio careers, side hustles and young people asking how they can maximise the value of their time.

Often that means becoming really good at something and then selling that skill for a few hours in a lot of places.

Our purpose at Sharesies is to create financial empowerment for everyone and there's still a lot to do in Aotearoa New Zealand, Australia and beyond.

We're focused on sharing opportunities and creating them where we can see they are missing. As we grow Sharesies, we see more and more doors that are closed to the majority of people. We're inspired to either create a new door to let people in, or to just smash it down.

It's a goal that keeps growing. Every time we think that we might have found a way to give people access to more chances to build their wealth, we find there's more to do.

These changes in mindset and technology have happened really quickly and there is so much more opportunity to come. We are confident that change is possible and the opportunities for the next generation are huge.

We're making really big steps towards our ambitions every day. If there was ever a time for change to be possible, it is now, with the use of technology and connectivity. We're all able to access financial markets via the phones in the palms of our hands — it's no longer just for people with access to the trading floors of stock exchanges.

It's so exciting and we hope that, through the course of this book, we've been able to share some tips to help you join us on our journey.

Your 10-step guide to getting started

We know some people flip straight to the back of a book and then go back and read the other chapters later (Brooke's one of those people). If you're just after a brief guide to getting started in share investing, here it is:

1. Accept that you can be an investor, right now, with whatever money you have available.

2. Work out how much you're going to invest to start off. Can you afford $5, $50, $50, $5000? Are you going to invest regularly (and did you know you can automate that)?

3. Plan your strategy. What are you investing in and why? Look at investing in companies and funds you care about. Use your money to make a statement about the world you want to see. Knowing why you've chosen what you've chosen is a really important part of being able to stick with it.

4. How much risk are you willing to tolerate with this investment? Think about how long you want your money to be invested for. Are your investments diversified? Consider whether you are investing across a range of industries and in different parts of the world.

5. What's your plan? Are you aiming to achieve a set amount of money, a particular return, or a certain amount of time in the market?

6. Don't be put off by market movements. When share prices drop, you're getting a bargain. Don't sell unless the investments in your portfolio no longer fit your needs or you've reached your goal. Panic-selling is one way that a lot of investors really short-change themselves.

7. Listen to news about your investments, but don't react

impulsively. Consider why you made your investment. Does the news change that reason? If not, stick to your strategy. Also, chat to your friends about what you're learning and doing. Make investing a normal part of your life, not a taboo subject.

8. Don't be swayed by FOMO, herd mentality or loss aversion. Acknowledge these normal human reactions, but keep referring back to your plan and your strategy. You don't need to buy a share just because everyone else is — and you definitely don't need to sell just because it feels like everyone else is, too.

9. Check in on your progress regularly, and alter your plans and goals if you need to. Stick with it. Time in the market is a huge asset.

10. Enjoy yourself. Investing should be an uplifting, optimistic experience.

Investor story: Sharing the knowledge

Sharon started investing in shares through her bank in 2010. At that time, there weren't many other options. She was in her mid-twenties, on an average income and only wanting to invest a couple of hundred dollars at a time.

The fees associated with the purchases made it pretty unsatisfying to begin with, because it took significant returns to cover the cost of having bought the shares, she says. She bought shares in a few companies, including Ryman Healthcare Limited (NZX:RYM) and Fisher & Paykel Healthcare Corporation Limited (ASX:FPH), and then largely forgot about them. Some of those investments are now worth 10 times what they initially cost and she wishes she had invested more money back then!

When the NZX started offering ETFs that investors could get into with a $500 initial payment and monthly contributions, Sharon started investing in a US mid-cap fund, too. The money slowly built over time without paying it much attention, and she mostly didn't worry about it very much.

Then, when Sharesies launched, Sharon jumped in. At first she made one-off payments into funds, then some individual companies, and the process is now totally automated with a regular monthly payment set to auto-invest in growth funds each time. She has also opened accounts for each of her kids.

'I feel like I've now actually built up a decent portfolio without feeling that I've had to sacrifice very much,' she says. 'I haven't sold anything except for some Xero (ASX:XRO) shares when I wanted a bit of cash to help supplement a deposit on my house. They'd grown in value a lot from when I bought them, so it was a nice surprise to be able to draw on them.'

Now, as a journalist of news website Stuff, she sees growing interest from readers in anything to do with investing, particularly in shares. 'It has been really noticeable over the course of my career that young people are increasingly into finding out about investment markets and how they can grow their financial wealth, particularly if they are locked out of property. This is leading to growing financial well-being — I think financial education without application isn't always useful but people are getting a chance to put what they learn into action, which is fantastic.'

Sharon plans to continue investing in shares alongside paying down her mortgage. Her long-term plan is to have the money available for her kids when they are older, to help them get off to a good start, and to supplement her KiwiSaver in retirement.

'I was shocking at maths at school,' she says, 'but I'm now really committed to helping people understand how the financial world works and how they can use it to get ahead.'

Glossary

Aggressive: This refers to an investing style that takes on a lot of risk, which should lead to more gains over the long term.

Assets: Things you own that have value. An asset could be money in the bank, a car, shares in a company, or a property.

Bear market: A general decline in the stock market over a period of time, as people move from feeling optimistic to more pessimistic about what might be ahead.

Bonds: A loan that you offer to a government or company. It's like an IOU — you give money in exchange for interest payments, and the promise of your money back at a certain point in time.

Bull market: A period of time on the sharemarket where lots of people are feeling confident and investing on the expectation that things will get better.

Capital gain: The profit you make when you sell an asset: the difference between the sale price and what you initially paid for it.

Dividend: Money paid to investors out of a company's profit. Dividend yield is the rate of return that investors are getting from a particular company through dividends. The dividend yield is calculated as the annual dividend paid divided by share price.

Float: The number of shares that are available to trade in any company.

Initial public offer (IPO): The process of offering the public the opportunity to invest in a company for the first time.

Hedging: An investment that's designed to reduce the risk of price movements, a bit like an insurance policy.

Index: A measure of a group of assets. We talk about the NZX50 or ASX50 index, which are the biggest 50 companies on the New Zealand and Australian exchanges.

Liquidity: How easy it is to sell an investment. A highly liquid investment is easy to get out of, like a bank account. A less liquid investment is something like a house, that requires a process to sell.

Market capitalisation: The total value of all of a company's issued shares.

Rebalance: Rebalancing is the process of reconfiguring an investment portfolio (or managed fund) to keep it in line with a desired target. If you had a fund that you wanted to be 50 per cent shares and 50 per cent cash, but then the shares performed really well and were suddenly worth more than 50 per cent of the fund, the fund manager would have to sell some shares to rebalance the fund back to 50:50.

Recession: Two consecutive quarters of a drop in economic activity.

Retail investors: Non-professional investors investing their own money. (People like you, probably.)

Shares: Small slices of a company owned by investors. Shares can be publicly traded, on a sharemarket, or owned privately. (You might also hear people talking about stocks and equities — these terms mean the same thing.)

Time horizon: The amount of time you have between buying your shares and needing the money back.